FOR THE LOVE OF MONEY

Human Behavior & Money

♡ $ ♡ $ ♡ $ ♡ $ ♡ $ ♡ $ ♡ $ ♡ $ ♡ $ ♡ $ ♡ $

FOR THE LOVE OF MONEY

♡ $ ♡ $ ♡ $ ♡ $ ♡ $ ♡ $ ♡ $ ♡ $ ♡ $ ♡ $ ♡ $

Human Behavior & Money

JAMES A. KNIGHT, MD

PROFESSOR OF PSYCHIATRY AND ASSOCIATE DEAN

TULANE UNIVERSITY SCHOOL OF MEDICINE

J. B. LIPPINCOTT COMPANY

Philadelphia - New York - Toronto

To

SALLY

*with more love
than money*

Preface

WHAT DOES MONEY MEAN to modern man? He earns, spends, and saves it. He dies for it; sometimes he kills for it. Why is man in bondage to this inanimate force, both creative and destructive, that can make a prince a pauper and a bum a baron?

One reads daily of charitable donations, of bank robberies, of inherited fortunes, occasionally of dollar bills found stuffed in old mattresses, and wonders about the personality traits, psychological problems and attitudes that express themselves through the medium of money.

For the Love of Money was stimulated by my psychiatric interest in the meaning of man's behavior toward money. It treats of the origins and analysis of such behavior in different age groups and circumstances.

The first two chapters deal with the psychological meaning and emotional uses of money, in normal, deviant, and adaptive behavior. The third chapter notes the important challenges in childrearing of introducing the child to money: let us remember that he carries into adulthood his childhood views of what money symbolizes. Chapter four continues the previous chapter, family ties often being fashioned of money or heavily influenced by it. The motives, meanings and methods of giving are discussed in chapter five, and extended to a discussion of altruism in chapter six. The final chapter focuses on the moral implications of man's concepts of money.

This material comes from many sources, across many boundaries that our increasing specialization has built around the separate disciplines and schools of thought. Although an eclectic approach to any subject contains both promise and danger, a subject that involves so many areas of human relationship demands it. Thus the material herein comes not only from the social and psychological sciences, but from philosophy and ethics as well.

This book may serve for many as a personal confrontation wherein their own attitudes toward money and its uses may be seriously reviewed. Since its concerns are shared by a variety of persons and groups, *For the Love of Money* is directed to an unrestricted audience. It may be of interest to fund raisers, bankers, and financiers, who seek and handle money, as well as to physicians, clergymen, psychiatrists, psychologists and social workers, who must repeatedly deal with the principles and practices of man's emotional uses of money. Hopefully, it will also speak to the bargain hunter, the gambler, the penny pincher, and to the parent whose offspring fantasies a money tree.

May it be for the professional a ready reference of psychological wisdom about money, and for the layman a contribution to understanding himself.

James A. Knight, MD

New Orleans
November, 1967

Acknowledgments

THE FIRST ENCOURAGEMENT for writing this book came
from Dr. Thomas K. Thompson, who, before he became
Director of Development, American Bible Society, was
executive director, Department of Stewardship and Benevolence, National Council of Churches. I participated
with him in a seminar on motivations in giving and the
psychological uses of money, and he urged me to do a
monograph on this topic. He has been generous with
his wise counsel, and I am deeply indebted to him.

Also, I am happy to express my gratitude to many
other friends and colleagues who helped in the preparation of this book. From them came ideas, illustrations,
suggestions for titles or chapter headings, editorial assistance, and enthusiastic encouragement. A few of the
many I want especially to thank are Dr. Lois DeBakey
and Mr. Bernard Saltzberg, my colleagues in the Tulane
School of Medicine; Dr. Ralph Slovenko, of the Menninger Foundation and the University of Kansas School
of Law; Dr. John L. Schimel, Associate Director and
Director of Clinical Services, the William Alanson White
Institute; Dr. Simon Doniger, editor of *Pastoral Psychology*; and Mrs. Lucile Seitzinger and Mrs. Carroll Wilson,
secretaries in Admissions at Tulane. A very special appreciation is reserved for my wife Sally, who contributed
immeasurably to every phase of the development of this
book. There are others, too numerous to mention, in
whose debt I stand for contributions tangible and
intangible.

Contents

The Psychological Meaning of Money

SYDNEY SMITH, the English clergyman and wit of the
late eighteenth and early nineteenth centuries, observed:
"I have been very poor the greater part of my life, and
have borne it as well, I believe, as most people, but I can
safely say that I have been happier every guinea I have
gained." This was an unorthodox statement for the
coming Victorian age, when the fiction was fashionable
that poverty and happiness went hand in hand. Such a
fiction enjoys no popularity in our time. Today poverty
is recognized as an evil and money as the potential means
of much good—of enjoying the arts, education, travel,
medical care, philanthropy, as well as the material necessities and comforts of life.

Each of us may understand the typical meaning of
money but simultaneously endow it with special significance. Hidden from the individual's conscious mind
will be some of the factors that shape its psychological
meaning for him.

Most people are concerned, more or less continu-
ously, consciously or unconsciously, with the solution
of their private money problems; for money, some
humans will do almost anything. Our concepts of
money influence our conduct, aspirations, and emotional reactions to ourselves, our families and friends.
The symbolic meaning of money to an individual is
determined by his cultural upbringing, religion, life ex-

11

periences, attitudes of parents and teachers, the examples of others, and by his short- and long-range goals.

MONETARY STRIVINGS

Satisfying One's Needs. A normal attitude toward money is to regard it as a means to an end and not as an end in itself. Money enables one to acquire certain things he needs and desires. Spending money is taken for granted as being necessary to security and self-confidence. The individual is aware that the more money he possesses, the better he can satisfy certain of his needs. This is surely rational. Otto Fenichel contends that if a person actually were disposed rationally, there would be no drive to become wealthy but only to meet requirements that he had learned to identify and assess through experience.[8] Although probably true, many men would still become wealthy as a by-product of their pursuit of other goals, many of which could be equally rational.

Not all people are given the same opportunity for the rational accumulation of money. A question often asked is how society succeeds in maintaining a state of affairs in which a large segment of its members are not able to satisfy their most basic needs, even when goods for their satisfaction are at hand in large quantities. Explosive uprisings attest to the impatience these deprived persons feel with present methods of finding a solution.

In general, however, peace is maintained, in one way or another. One method is by force, penal justice or, at times, "penal injustice." Another method is by nurturing in people the drive to become wealthy. Deprivations are easier to bear when they are coupled with dreams of a better future. One can bear the sight of better-situated people more easily when he feels the psychological possibility of identification with them. Society's ideal of *thrift* serves to obscure the true class relationships, and to create illusions concerning the possibilities of personal social advancement. Fortunately, though, the ferment of social mobility serves to dissolve many such illusions, and racial unrest forces reexamination and change.

Quest for Emotional Security. Money has a powerful effect on our inner feelings of anxiety. In a world of turmoil and sudden change, the quest for money is motivated greatly by the desire to find something akin to a magical charm for attaining emotional security. The quest then moves the individual into competitive struggles where success becomes his form of self-validation.

Individual competitive success may well be the dominant goal in our culture, in large cities and in small towns. This goal is not limited to economic activity, although there it receives its clearest definition. Individual competitive success is given top priority as a cultural value because it is identified with self-esteem and self-worth; it is to the modern man what religious salvation was to the citizens of the Middle Ages. Success in our day is a matter essentially not of achieving material gain but acquiring security, in that the success is accepted as a proof of one's power, in the eyes of oneself and others. In such a value system, unfortunately, economic gain becomes personal valuation.

This competitive striving for success also involves a serious effort to triumph over others, thus augmenting intrasocial hostility and interpersonal isolation. Since one's own success is relative to that of others', such a cultural value is insatiable. A person's failure to achieve competitive success earns for him not only social contempt but, more important, self-contempt and feelings of worthlessness. The same pertains to the college student who flunks out.

Yet on this competitive striving we depend for our security. Even a relatively minor trauma—a stock market fluctuation—is experienced by many as a catastrophic event, a threat to values held essential to their existence as personalities. Such individuals experience profound anxiety. Since success is their chief form of self-validation, feelings of anxiety generally lead them to redouble their efforts. It is obvious, then, that anxiety growing out of their competitive striving leads to more competitive striving and to more anxiety.

Here one cannot help thinking of the Calvinistic ethic and its impact on modern business practices. With Calvinism came the view that success (proved by profit) was the certain indication that the chosen vocation was pleasing to God, and also that dislike of work was considered a sign of failure displeasing to God. The ethic permitted, even consecrated, the effort to become wealthy, and probably for the first time wealth was reconciled with a good conscience.

Modern man's top cultural goals have increased his psychological isolation and enhanced his individualism. His efforts to create new forms of relatedness have failed. His anxiety drives him to a variety of attempts to overcome his isolation. The development of adequate forms of community life is the antidote to anxiety that modern man would like to attain, but his cultural values interfere and block its attainment.

Students of human behavior see widespread anxiety about money in almost all types of people and age groups. What are the earliest roots of this anxiety? Is it related to some anticipation of privation as experienced in childhood? Very young children, in the course of their experiences with accidents and illnesses, come to associate these with the worried speech and anxious appearance of their parents. The parents' behavior arouses the children's anxiety. If parents speak and act similarly concerning money problems, then possibly the child's feelings of anxiety will also be transferred to the topic of money, especially the lack of it. Acquiring money would supposedly reduce this anxiety, and the behavior that resulted from obtaining money would therefore be strongly reinforced and later adopted by the child. With sufficient exposure to this type of experience, a child could become highly motivated to obtain money or economic success. The underlying motive, however, even though other drives might be present, would be to reduce anxiety. Such an interpretation of the motive behind money-making is consistent with the view commonly held that many motives are not what they seem on the surface. When behavior that results from such motives successfully reduces fear and anxiety, then one tends further to utilize it.

The Will to Power. Seventy-five years ago, the Reverend Russell Herman Conwell, a Philadelphia Baptist minister, went about the nation delivering a popular speech, "Acres of Diamonds." He proclaimed to his audience that securing wealth is an honorable ambition, and is one test of a person's usefulness to others.

Money is power. Every good man and woman ought to strive for power, to do good with it when obtained. I say, get rich, get rich!

Conwell gave the same speech before 6,000 audiences and proved his point by earning eight million dollars. If he had lived to see the United States today, he would find thousands of people following his counsel, although many of them have never heard of Conwell and his "Acres of Diamonds."

Appraisal by business authorities reveals that in no other country of the world at no other time in history have the chances to make a fortune been better than right now. Government estimates show that in recent years millionaires have been increasing at the rate of 5,000 a year; *US News and World Report* estimates that millionaires in our country now number 90,000. The idea is fallacious that great fortunes are a thing of the past, and that income and inheritance taxes have wiped out millionaires who survived the Depression. Millionaires have increased 300% during the past decade, while the population has increased only 20%.

In numerous studies of millionaires who have recently acquired their fortunes, the point is made that the newly rich respect the power of money and are aware of what it can buy. The power rests particularly in the mobility and creativity that money brings to enable the rich to become richer. The possessor of money in our society is honored and powerful. First Friedrich Nietzsche and then Alfred Adler spoke of "the will to power"; the drive to become wealthy seems to be related. Why should one aspire to the feeling of being powerful, of enjoying respect or honor? The "will to power" is identical with a high "level of self-regard." Such a goal has its origin in the fact that young children feel themselves omnipotent, and that throughout their lives a certain memory of this omnipotence remains, with a longing to attain it again.

The problems of self-regard and its fluctuations have been discussed definitively by Sandor Rado.[22] In his narcissism, the infant feels omnipotent but later on learns that his power is limited. The longing to attain once again this lost sense of omnipotence persists throughout life. A high degree of self-regard means coming close to the lost feeling of omnipotence, and a low degree means remoteness from it. The child feels a diminution of his self-regard if he loses the affection of others, and a rise if he gains affection. The need is the baby's hunger, its satisfaction the baby's satiety.

The psychoanalytic view is that the child retains a strong belief in omnipotence after the loss of his own, by regarding as all-powerful the persons who limit his omnipotence. In fact, the child may try to exercise an even greater omnipotence by seeking to control and manipulate the omnipotent persons around him. To get something from them means to be reunited with them and *to participate in their power*. To be rejected by them means to be reduced to helplessness. This dependence on external supplies of love, warmth and food makes the child amenable to training. To receive these indispensable supplies, the child must abstain from expressing certain instinctual impulses regarded by his parents as undesirable, and behave in an approved manner. The promise to the helpless of protection and power, conditional on the observance of certain moral regulations, is encountered later at various points in social life.

The promise of protection and power is also found in religion: God promises protection, help, and some participation in His power to the helpless human being— provided he fulfills certain ethical requirements. Religion, to an unfortunate extent, is a "bargaining" between man and his God. A more acceptable theological word is "covenant."

Acquiring wealth appears to be a means of increasing, or preventing a lowering of, the level of one's self-regard. This need can be viewed as a derivative of the primitive form of regulation of self-regard in which the individual feeds his ego from the environment in the same way in which he, as an infant, required an external supply of food. Money, then, is an ego-supplement, and the possibility of getting rich—the idea of being wealthy—becomes an ideal. The attainment of wealth is fantasied and worked for as something bound up with an enormous increase of self-regard.

Thus the original and basic aim is not for riches, but to enjoy power and respect among one's fellow men or within oneself. In our society, power and respect are mostly based on the possession of money; this makes the need for power and respect a need for riches. For many people, the full realization of their potentialities means becoming a financial success. Money then serves as a medal of life's achievement. The accumulation of money becomes the chief aim and the mark of a life well spent. If a large sum of money is not acquired, one becomes a failure to himself and others.

In the realm of power and money, the sexual dimension may enter into certain behavioral patterns. For kleptomaniacs, or for women who strive to drain men of their resources, money symbolizes a whole series of things that have been withheld from them. During periods of competition with the mother for the love of the father, the little girl never forgets those special gifts, no matter how trivial, that her mother received from her father. The painful memories of these experiences are hidden away in the deeper recesses of the mind. Her behavior is an effort, though not conscious, to even the score with mother and father.

Rado assigns to the kleptomaniac and the vamp similar dynamics, pleasure in stealing and exploitation.[21] He states that the kleptomaniac endows the object stolen, usually worthless to her, with great emotional value. She is acquiring a symbol of power in an effort to strengthen her feelings of weakness, which she has retained since childhood. The vamp's behavior is designed fundamentally to capture the man's power. The financial trophy (money) assures the woman that she has conquered the enemy and appropriated his power. These women figuratively drain men dry. They cause men to become infatuated with them by using the most childish tricks and flattery, very much like those which children are accustomed to use with their mothers.

When one examines the cases of certain prostitutes, as well as of their pimps and customers who fulfill the function of supply and demand, money as power may come strongly into play. Money in our society is a symbol of virile power, and a girl can play the part of Delilah. The prostitute who takes money away from the man may be, in her unconscious mind, castrating him. At the same time the man who pays for using as he pleases a woman's body treats her as merchandise, thereby degrading her and taking away something of her soul.

To some men, money is a symbol of their potency. They regard any loss of money as a loss or threat of loss of their masculinity, as a castration. Often, when a man is in danger, he may sacrifice money in a kind of "prophylactic self-castration."[8]

In the great biblical hymn of creation, man is given dominion over the beasts of the field, the birds of the air and the fishes of the sea. This commission assigns him great power and authority, and man has taken this trust a step further and sought power as an end in itself —for example, the power to hoard. Such a will to power often places undue value on money, a potential power ready for action at any time and able to assume almost any possible form. Few people recognize the blasphemy of the casually used term "almighty dollar." It is understandable that money has been compared to primitive *mana*, because of its quantitative, potential character of pure power.

Mana, a word of Polynesian derivation, is looked on as extraphysical power immanent in and emanating from nature. It is viewed as the embodiment of all elemental forces that, taken together, produce and maintain the order of the universe. Mana is manifested in many ways—by prophetic vision, magical power, authority and prestige. In depth psychology, mana carries the meaning of psychic energy, which wells up from the unconscious and infuses the personality with great spiritual power.

Usually, the advantages of power that a man is able to procure for himself and his dependents bear some relationship to his talents, personal character and competence. By means of money, however, success, advantages and power can be completely divorced from personal inherent qualities. The person who has inherited money, the manipulator who has been fortunate with his speculations, and even the lucky one who has hit the jackpot, enjoy the same advantages and power as the man who has acquired his money by hard work. Unfortunately, when the power of money is associated with incompetence or lack of character, its disastrous effects can ruin other people as well as the owner.

Another destructive dimension to the power of money is the ease with which wealth in terms of money can be measured. Money then becomes the standard by which every kind of wealth is judged, its possession the ideal of most people. The inevitable consequence is that of shifting the evaluation of social relationships from the personal to the impersonal. In his letter to Timothy, Paul stated: "The love of money is the root of all evil" (I Tim. 6:10). The insight of the biblical writers is amazingly current in that obsession with money is the worst form of demonic possession, and that to set supreme value on acquiring money is a total service to Mammon. Commitment to money as an end in itself has made the high-pressure salesman the soul of commerce. The cycle is set in motion by someone wanting to acquire money. He looks around for some means of raising it, perhaps by making something he can "force" on the buyer. The article he produces may bring him no pride of creative fulfillment, but regardless of what he is producing, he must proclaim his wares until people are convinced they must buy them, and then, his objective is achieved.

Possessions: Expanded Portion of Self. In the deeper layers of the mind, money, like all other possessions, assumes the role of parts of the body one could lose or, after the fantasy that they have been lost, wishes to regain. Fenichel, in tracing the etymology of the word "possession," states that "possession is that upon which one sits."[8] It is often said that the miser sits on his money. Karl Abraham tells how his dog used to sit on objects, such as bones, that he regarded as his possessions.[1] "Squatter's rights" is a meaningful phrase almost anywhere in the world, and nearly everyone refers to his savings account as a nest egg.

One of Aesop's fables is about a miser who sold all he had and bought a lump of gold, which he buried in a hole by the side of a wall. Daily he went to look at it. One of his workmen observed his visits and, on digging down, discovered the gold and stole it. The miser, on his next visit, found the hole empty and began to make loud lamentations. Seeing his grief and learning of his loss, a neighbor encouraged him to place a stone in the hole and fancy that the gold was still lying there. The neighbor assured him that this would do him the same service, for when the gold was there he had not the slightest intention of using it.

What is the unconscious meaning of the real or fantasied action of sitting on certain objects? The motivation seems to be related to the fear that these objects could be taken away. The infant confuses the objects around him with himself. At first, he probably thinks his mother's breast is actually a part of himself; gradually, he so discovers his own body that it begins to seem set apart from the rest of his environment. Later, he possesses articles of property in the same way he possesses his own body. Thus possessions become an expanded portion of the self.

In the early stages of childhood, the child has the idea that he would like to put everything that is pleasurable into his mouth and swallow it, and spit out everything that is painful. He soon learns that many pleasurable things cannot be taken into his mouth. Those things, sooner or later, are called *mine*. Thus, symbolically, his possessions are things that he would like to be a part of himself. Possession means things that do not actually belong to the self but ought to— things that are actually outside the person, but symbolically inside. Although they are in the outside world, they are invested with feeling and significance to the point of their becoming a part of one's ego. Possessions are generally provided with certain attributes for the purpose of identifying them. Thus a person will say, "The red one belongs to me." All money looks alike, so it is a deindividualized possession, and thus capable of being lost. Therefore, money is watched over as a possession constantly in danger of losing the quality "of belonging to me."

In the study of human behavior, it is impressive to see how the relationships of biologic and sociologic data are intertwined. The inclination to possession is a derivative of bodily love, and can be an overcompensation for fear of loss of parts of the body. The drive to accumulate money, which seems to be a special form of the need for possession, is made possible by the social function of money. Because of this, the need to accumulate becomes a special form of bodily narcissism and an expression of the fear of bodily injury. We have all heard both men and women say: "I feel naked without my pocketbook." Fingert has reported that one of his patients whose reluctance to use his own money to pay treatment fees was related to a fear of losing part of his own body.[10] Although the patient could pay for his treatment, he was reticent in discussing financial matters, and insisted that his father pay for the treatment as a means of avoiding inheritance taxes. When he expressed his anger at being forced to discuss money at the beginning of treatment, protesting that it was unimportant, he was advised to pay for his psychoanalytic therapy in cash rather than by check. He began to discuss his hoarding and tried to continue to pay by check. When told again that it would be better to pay in cash, he responded with the most intense emotion yet revealed in his psychoanalysis. Through an examination of his hostility, it became evident that reluctance to use his own money was related to a fear of losing part of his body. This fear was also manifested in other aspects of his behavior.

The fear of bodily injury that causes the body to strive continually for the insurance of its integrity and protection is usually called "castration anxiety." The name is taken from the most important form of fear of bodily injury, the fear of genital injury, which develops because of sexual feelings and activity in the early stages of psychosexual development in both sexes, but especially in the male. Today, the term "castration fear" is used, in a general sense, to refer to fear of injury of any part of the body integrity.

The symbol of the dragon and the myths surrounding it show how deeply rooted are the relationships of possessions and the self. The dragon is often portrayed guarding the treasures hidden in a cave or vault. Ascribed to the dragon are such characteristics as strength, vigilance, exceptionally keen eyesight, and animal traits considered aggressive and dangerous. Because of these characteristics, in ancient times the dragon was given the task of guarding treasures and temples. Present-day psychology defines the dragon-symbol as something terrible to overcome, and he who conquers the dragon becomes the hero. In a way, the dragon could be symbolic of the instincts. When one conquers the dragon, he conquers the primitive and instinctual side of himself. The treasure that the hero wins only after painful effort may be himself reborn.

This may be taken a step further with jewels and gems. Jewels have signified spiritual truths, and precious stones or gems superior knowledge. Thus the treasures guarded by dragons allude to the conflicts and pain in the struggle for knowledge of self and the wisdom of living. When one acquires this treasure, he has indeed attained richness. This is especially true when one realizes that in many Indian and Chinese legends the Great Dragon hides in his maw a beautiful diamond that gives immortality. The hero kills the dragon in order to take away the precious stone of immortality.

SYMBOL OF RELATIONSHIP AND BELONGING

One of the deepest of man's longings is to enter fully into a shared life with others. In this lofty sense, despite the slavery and oppression that existed in early

Greece and Rome, money symbolized the loving giving and taking among individuals that gave men the feeling of having emotional roots in their community. Desmonde contends that money can be regarded as a quest, a search for emotional unity in group psychology, which persists even in the face of injustice and evil.[5] This longing for mutual devotion is basic within the heart of every man, and the history of money is the story of the forms that this yearning has taken.

The excellent studies and clinical observations of the ill effects on a young child of maternal deprivation of food, love, or warmth are numerous. The way in which his elemental needs are met probably influences the child's later attitudes toward money. When deprived of loving care, the child tends to lack the capacity for entering into loving and moral relationships with others in later life. His ability to give and receive affection is crippled, and he is unable to understand and accept the necessity for imposing limitations on his own desires. Psychoanalysis has shown that the pathological quest for money is often closely associated with the maternal image.[12] The mothering person is essential for the survival of the infant. The same conditions that make the infant long for a mother's love continue to exist, although on a different level, when he becomes an adult. If the individual could find *mother* for the rest of his years, life would be relieved of many of its uncertainties and misfortunes. It is no small surprise then that man is driven to pursue this mirage and find in money a substitute for mother.

The father, also, plays a major role. As the provider of food, he sets an example of dedicated sharing and loyal interdependence. Many of the child's first conceptions of money and the division of labor are received from the efforts and sacrifices made by his father and mother for his welfare. The very essence of money is related to the joy in giving to others and the capacity to appreciate gifts. These moral insights are first learned from parents.

In studies of prostitutes, it is not uncommon to find a history of severe parental deprivation in their childhood. Prostitution becomes the vehicle for their search for someone who would care for them in the way that they had not been cared for originally. The money they receive is seen as a symbol for the warmth, love, and food that they had craved but had not received in their early years. It is understandable that their slang word for money is bread. It seems, however, that the money is usually an unsatisfactory substitute and is usually squandered or given away to a pimp in a further effort to find a gratifying emotional relationship.

The person who is chronically depressed or prone to have depressions often equates money with food. Human conceptions of food, the basic economic commodity, are the prototype of attitudes toward the functioning of the money institution. In many ways, the early history of money is largely the history of the meaning of food for man. Desmonde writes that the common meal was the first "money" in our culture, and that this shared food was at the core of the social institutions of Greek and Roman antiquity.[5] Eating food in common represented to ancient man sharing a vital power, participating in a mutual source of strength. Possibly the love feast was also the origin of the Eucharist.

In the distant past, if when entering a castle the visitor was given bread and salt, this was assurance that he would be protected during his stay and his throat would not be cut.

The hero in a primitive community is frequently the

person most proficient in obtaining food for his group. Success in the quest for food, Richards states, "determines almost universally social prestige in a savage society. . . . Such success may depend either on individual qualities—endurance, daring and patient concentration—or the attainment of special skill and facility." [23]

For ancient man, food was a sacred ritual in which the sharers renewed their creative commitment by reidentifying themselves with a common source of strength and energy. Obtaining food under conditions of peril was an expression of heroism and honor. Participating in the shared food was equivalent to receiving a medal for courage and devotion. In the legend of King Arthur and his Knights of the Round Table, only those who had proved themselves in specific traits of character were accepted as members of the communion.

Our fragmented society has isolated man. He finds it difficult to share with others for essentially the same reason that a starving man finds it difficult to share his food. The struggle to accumulate wealth may be an effort to neutralize and escape a pathologic fear of impoverishment, growing partly out of man's sense of isolation. An analysis of the fear of impoverishment reveals that the loss of possession and the loss of love that are feared, mean a loss of self-regard, a diminution of power, and a return to the status of a helpless, hungry child. Kahlil Gibran, in *The Prophet*, has asked the crucial question: "Is not dread of thirst when your well is full, the thirst that is unquenchable?" [13]

In reality, money is a symbol of the emotional relations between an individual and the other members of his group. It is the record of a complex system comprised of rights and correlative promises arising out of human actions in the past and human faith in the future.[24] Much in our society is based on these promises; the word "credit" means "faith." To a great extent, money has become a record of interpersonal promises. This is even more understandable when we realize that most of our transactions are carried on by checks, or even 'phone calls, and that a large part of the money in existence, such as savings accounts, bonds, and insurance policies, exists merely in the form of records in the office of business concerns. Thus the symbol of money, regardless of its form, is a seal of good faith, marking society's indebtedness to an individual for his services to the community.

Monetary transactions, as records of interpersonal promises, probably enhance the almost priestly tradition of banks. Many of the older banks have huge and formal entrances, vaulted interiors, and solemn marble columns. Presidents of banks are usually held in awe. The bank and its president suggest to many the temple and its priest.

This is not a far-fetched relationship when one remembers that from the earliest days of Babylon, the temple was the repository for money. The priests were the bankers in Babylonia, and later in Greece and Rome, and conducted business similar to many of the activities of the modern bank. Also, they stored gold and valuables in their vaults and accepted deposit fees.

The first Egyptian bankers and the earliest English moneychangers conducted their business sitting on a bench, customarily located in a courtyard of the temple. It was from this type of temple-bank that Christ drove the moneychangers (John 2:14-17; Matthew 21:12; Mark 11:15; Luke 19:45). Our word for *bank* comes from *bench*.

The word *money* had its origin in religious roots. In Roman mythology, Juno Regina was the wife of Jupiter and queen of the heavens. Because of her watchfulness and protective qualities, she became known as the goddess of warning. The Romans built a temple to Juno on the Capitoline Hill as an expression of gratitude to her for warning them on numerous occasions about dangers ahead. When coinage was devised they placed their mint in her temple; as Juno Moneta, the goddess became the guardian of the finances. Her name *Moneta* was derived from the Latin word *moneo*, "warn," and finally entered Old French as *moneie* and much later became our word money. Actually, through another route the word *moneta* came into Old English as *mynet*, which was transformed into the word *mint*, that place where money was made.

STATUS, REDEMPTION, AND IMMORTALITY

Besides intellectual and artistic achievement, money remains one of the few means of acquiring a respectable and respected social status. It is a natural and commendable part of human nature for persons to try to actualize their intellectual and emotional powers by seeking the social position that will enable them to exercise their creative capacities to a greater degree. Unfortunately, all the aspirants to a particular position in a social group are not qualified to succeed in their goals. The irrational side of human nature manifests itself in the quest for the unattainable position within the division of labor, and this is a source of much injustice and unhappiness.

Our strange values regarding money and status have been pointedly attacked by Lord Keynes:

When the accumulation of wealth is no longer of high social importance, there will be great changes in the code of morals. We shall be able to rid ourselves of many of the pseudo-moral principles which have hag-ridden us for two hundred years, by which we have exalted some of the most distasteful of human qualities into the position of the highest virtues. We shall be able to afford to dare to assess the money-motive at its true value. The love of money as a possession—as distinguished from the love of money as a means to the enjoyments and realities of life—will be recognized for what it is, a somewhat disgusting morbidity, one of those semi-criminal, semi-pathological propensities which one hands over with a shudder to the specialists in mental disease.[16]

Loewenstein states that money has held more varied significance for the Jews than for most people.[19] Many of the Jewish temporal aspirations have centered on money because of the lack of other outlets. For several centuries money represented their only means of surviving persecution and expulsion, and this is again true today—for them, as well as for others in areas of political upheaval.

Amar, discussing money from a socioanalytic point of view, reaches the conclusion that money has become the main instrument in man's quest for self-punishment and in his attempts at redemption from his feelings of guilt.[3] He points out, further, that for the man in the street, money is above everything else a source of worry. Most transactions regarding money are done in an aggressive context. While money in the beginning represented value, production, and riches, it has now become a symbol and convention. It is always owed to someone even if it is only to one's self. Amar states that the basic accounting principles are that *he who receives owes, and the more one owns, the more one owes.*

Whence in such a situation can redemption come? The advent of science has led to the transformation of God into a human phenomenon. Science has discarded the notion of original sin and the possibility of discharging guilt feelings by religious rituals; this burden has been taken up partly by our notions about money. Unconscious feelings about original sin, impossible redemption, cosmic catastrophes and hell are now transposed to an economic context. Amar points out that an economic crash, like that of 1929, clearly shows that money does not represent a reality, such as products and productivity, but reveals the irrational element in our economic structure. The crash, according to him, did not happen because something went wrong in the capitalistic system. Crashes and recessions will occur even though the system works exactly as it is supposed to, because it has in itself a seed for autodestruction, which Amar traces back to unconscious guilt. The state has become the supreme creditor whom the debtor can never satisfactorily repay.

Feldman has studied patients who dream of finding money.[7] In a typical dream, a patient finds in the sand on a road an almost endless supply of coins. Analysis of such dreams reveals that the coins symbolized the life of the dreamer and the denial of death: "Life cannot be destroyed, it will go on indefinitely." Of course, one's cultural traditions furnish material for dreams. At Jewish funerals in Central Europe, coins are collected in a metal box; the collector chants: "Charity saves you from death." On leaving the cemetery, each mourner pours water from a jar on his hands and the water falls into a container into which coins are dropped, signifying the imperishability of life. The custom among Jews in Central Europe for a departing guest to give "parting money" to the children is also interpreted as an attempt by the guest to deny death and to attain immortality by remaining in the memory of the children.

Brown contends that "life remains a war against

death—civilized man, no more than archaic man, is not strong enough to die—and death is overcome by accumulating time-defying monuments. These accumulations of stone and gold make possible the discovery of the immortal soul."[4] Perhaps it is not an accident, says Keynes in his profound appraisal of economic behavior, that the group that did the most to bring the promise of immortality into the heart of man has also done most for the principle of compound interest.[16] The ambition of civilized man is revealed in the pyramid, the achievement of the first modern individualists. In the pyramid reside both the hope of immortality and the fruit of compound interest. Where money and immortality were once primarily the pursuit of kings, they are now also the pursuit of the common man.

Unfortunately, the immortality of an estate or a corporation resides in the dead things that alone endure. The last stage of history is, as Luther said, the dominion of death in life. Possibly all men spend their lives conquering death, whether in economic or other forms of activity. At the end of the third of his Odes, Horace writes: "I have wrought a monument more enduring than bronze, and loftier than the royal accumulation of the pyramids. Neither corrosive rain nor raging wind can destroy it, nor the innumerable sequence of years nor the flight of time. I shall not altogether die."[4]

FILTHY LUCRE

Both the biblical record and psychoanalytic writing testify to man's distortions of the real value of money. Filthy lucre as used in the Bible (for example: I Timothy 3:8, Titus 1:7, 11; I Peter 5:2) refers to "base gain," or to the fact that money is often the means of prostituting human personality. William Tyndale, in his translation of the New Testament from Greek into

English, translated "base gain" as *filthy lucre,* and later the King James Version retained it. The implication is not that money is filthy or evil in itself; the filthiness or evil is in the man who is misusing it, not in the money. One can understand, then, the biblical warning: "The love of money is the root of all evil" (I Timothy 6:10).

Long before the Christian era, West Aryan tribesmen employed the word *leu* to stand for profit or gain. The Romans began to use it as *lucrum* to designate wages as well as profit. For a long period of history the term was highly respectable. Today, *filthy lucre* is sometimes jocularly used for money or for gain, profit and pecuniary advantage. Usually, however, it has only an unfavorable implication: gain viewed as a low motive of action; for centuries it has carried this connotation. Good illustrations are the statements in Addison's *Tatler:* "I did not make that judgment for the sake of filthy lucre," and in Kingsley's *Yeast:* "The last place in which he will look for the cause of his misery is in that very money-mongering to which he now clings as frantically as ever."[17]

Here a retrospective view of the mechanics of money may help us. Money is thought to have originated out of religious and social custom rather than directly out of a system of bartering or exchanging goods. Commodities, which later came to be important as a standard of value or medium of exchange, seem first to have been important as ransom, bride-price, ceremonial offering, or means of ostentation. Thus, the application to economic ends generally developed out of the earlier discharge of religious, legal and ritualistic uses. Any such system, however, has its difficulties because of the lack of proper standards to value each object. Then an instrument called money gradually evolved, to be used in measuring and exchanging, one with another, those natural riches by means of which men most easily supply their necessities. Surely, it must be recognized that all money is artificial wealth, for a man may have an abundance of it and die of hunger. Such a possibility is illustrated by the covetous and fabled king of Phrygia called Midas, to whom Bacchus granted the wish that whatever he touched might become gold. He begged, later, that this boon be withdrawn to prevent his perishing from hunger and thirst. Many who have sought wealth have discovered, like Midas, that money does not always meet the needs of human life, but is only an artificial instrument devised to facilitate the exchange of natural riches.

As through the centuries man has emphasized that money in itself has no intrinsic value, so has psychoanalytic doctrine. Most of the psychoanalytic writings on money have emphasized the relationship of money and—is it strange?—excrement. Norman O. Brown brings the issue in focus: "In its famous paradox, the equation of money and excrement, psychoanalysis becomes the first science to state what common sense and the poets have long known—that the essence of money is its absolute worthlessness."[4] This view, long a part of the biblical tradition and of the wisdom of man in general, was seized on by Freud in spelling out the equation: money equals excreta.[11] Freud described how certain personality types may misuse money as an expression of their underlying character traits. Although his findings cannot be accepted as indisputable, they add another dimension to the understanding of the individual.

From earliest infancy, the human being goes through stages of development. Even a casual reading of Spock's book,[26] or the observation of a child in one's home, gives convincing evidence of this. According to psycho-analytic formulations, the infant feels a kind of vague pleasure over his entire body when he is handled by his mother or others. However, certain areas, the eroto-genic zones, take up a large quantity of pleasurable feeling. Three such zones merit emphasis: the oral (or mouth), the anal, and the genital. First, the concentra-tion of feeling is in the mouth and lips, most pro-nounced during the first year of life. As the infant gets a little older, the area of special sensitivity shifts to the anal region, and remains there during the second and third years. With further development, the libido or psychic energy is concentrated in the third or genital area, where it gradually evolves into adult sexuality. This phase constitutes the fourth and fifth years of life.

Erik Erikson has broadened the base of Freud's psy-chosocial stages by tying this theory of infantile sex-uality to our present-day knowledge of the child's phys-ical and social growth within his family and the social structure.[6] The first year of life he calls the stage of basic trust, the second and third years the stage of autonomy, and the fourth and fifth years the stage of initiative.

Our major concern here is the stage of autonomy, which corresponds in Freudian theory to the anal stage. Psychoanalysis uses the word "anality" to designate the particular pleasurableness and willfulness that often attach at this stage to the eliminative organs. Evacuat-ing the bowels and the bladder is enhanced from the beginning by a premium of feeling good. In the young child, this premium must make up for frequent dis-comfort and tension suffered as the bowels learn to do their daily work. As the muscle system develops, the child learns "to hold" and "to let go"; a general ability seems to develop in the child to drop and to throw away, and to alternate withholding and expelling at will.

Thus, toilet training now becomes the most obviously disturbing item of child training in the widest circles of our society. It is usually assumed that early and vigorous training is absolutely necessary for the kind of personality that will function efficiently in a mechanized world, which says "time is money" and calls for orderliness, punctuality, and thrift. Possibly we have gone too far, with this type of training, in assuming that a child is an animal that must be broken, and some of the psychological problems we see in patients may be related to this training. Notwithstanding, our clinical work suggests that the "overcompulsive" type—stingy, retentive, and meticulous in matters of affection, time, and money, as well as in matters concerning the bowels—is not rare among the neurotics frequently seen.

In the child, the anal zone lends itself well to the expression of stubborn insistence on conflicting impulses. It is the ideal instrument at the child's disposal for alternating or contradictory modes—for retention or elimination. Thus this stage of child development becomes a battle for autonomy. If outer control by too rigid or too early parental training insists on robbing the child of his attempt gradually to control his bowels and other functions willingly and by his free choice, he will counter with rebellion against his parents and a deep sense of inner defeat. Erikson has clearly stated the issue of this stage: from a *sense of self-control without loss of self-esteem* comes a lasting sense of autonomy and pride; but from a sense of muscular and anal impotence, of loss of self-control and of parental overcontrol comes a lasting sense of doubt and shame.[6]

A child usually progresses smoothly, but with considerable overlap, from one stage of psychosocial development to the next. If his growth has been interfered with, the child may remain partly arrested or fixed in one of these stages and not move on to psychological maturity. Much of what psychoanalysis has contributed to the study of money is related to the partial bondage of the person to the anal stage of his development, the stage of toilet training, particularly in our culture. The concentration of emotional energy in the anal zone by the child may have a lasting effect. It is not difficult to understand how excessive attention and preoccupation by the mother on a particular area of the child's socialization may confuse the child and lead him to place undue emphasis on a simple biologic process. Part of this psychic energy later becomes attached to the habits and disciplines identified with toilet training (regularity of stool, etc.). Thus regularity of action subsequently becomes incorporated in the personality without conscious recognition of its original manifestation. Regularity, punctuality and allied character traits have their origins in training during the second and third years of life, at which time the groundwork for law and order is laid in the child's mind.

In "Character and Anal Erotism," Freud asserts the relationship of money and excrement as reflected in both our conscious and unconscious thought processes.[11] Two of his conclusions, derived from clinical experience with patients, suggest that personality traits may become profoundly modified as the result of relief of tension experienced by the infant in the region of the anal canal, and that an association exists between character type and anal activity. Freud confined himself to the three character traits that are most typically related to a fixation at the toilet training stage of psychosocial development: orderliness, parsimony and obstinacy.[11]

The traits of cleanliness, orderliness and reliability Freud explains as reactions against an interest in things that are unclean and intrusive and ought not to be on the body. Orderliness also covers the notion of trust-worthiness and conscientiousness in carrying out small duties. Obstinacy grows out of the "battle of the nursery," the struggles between mother and child in toilet training as the child expresses his autonomy and the mother seeks to control and train the child. The obstinacy can go over into defiance, to which rage and revengefulness are easily joined. Parsimony may appear in the exaggerated form of avarice.

Freud goes on to say that the connections that exist between the two complexes of interest in money and activities of the toilet, which seem so dissimilar, appear to be most far-reaching:

In reality, whenever archaic modes of thought predominate or have persisted—in ancient civilizations, in myth, fairy tale and superstition, in unconscious thoughts and dreams, and in the neuroses—money comes into the closest relation with excrement. We know how the money which the devil gives his paramours turns into excrement after his depar-ture and the devil is most certainly nothing more than a personification of the unconscious instinctual forces. The superstition, too, which associates the finding of treasure with defecation is well known, and everyone is familiar with the figure of the "excretor of ducats" (*Dukatenscheis-ser*). Even in the Babylon cult, gold is the "excrement of Hell." [11]

Many stories and linguistic expressions point to the association between money and feces. The "excretor of ducats" (gold-bug) story is a fairy tale equivalent to the goose that laid the golden egg. We speak of a man "rolling" or "wallowing" in money, of the man who is "stinking rich," of the dirty or filthy miser.* And on the stock exchange, a man who is hard up is said to be constipated. Although other examples from many walks of life could demonstrate further the relationship of money to feces, the vocabulary of the gambler is especially descriptive. The stakes are "the pot," and the player refers to making "a big pot" or to "cleaning up." Dice are called "craps," and a lucky player is often one who has fallen into "a barrel of crap." Losing is "being cleaned out," winning "making a killing." When one looks at his hand slowly, he is "squeezing out a hand."

Ernest Jones, in "Anal-erotic Character Traits," declares that the sense of value attached to money is a direct continuation of the sense of value that the infant attaches to his excretory product. In the adult, this latter concern is banished into the unconscious and is replaced by a conscious attachment to money.[15]

Sandor Ferenczi traces the stages by which the child passes from the original idea of excrement to the apparently remote one of money.[9] Experience gathered from observation of the behavior of children and psychoanalytic investigation of neurotics suggests that children originally devote their interest without any inhibition to the process of defecation, and that it affords them pleasure to hold back their stools. "The

* In Frank Norris' *McTeague*, a character named Trina gives dramatic testimony to the need or tendency literally to roll in money. She obtained from her uncle the five thousand dollars he was holding for her. One evening she spread all the gold pieces between the sheets and then went to bed naked. All night she slept on the money, taking a strange and ecstatic pleasure in the touch of the smooth flat pieces along the length of her entire body. On other occasions she would lie on the bed and gather the gleaming heaps of gold pieces to her with both arms, burying her face in them with long sighs of unspeakable delight. Her passion for her money had excluded every other sentiment.

excremata thus held back are really the first 'savings' of the growing being, and as such remain in a constant, unconscious interrelationship with every bodily activity or mental striving that has anything to do with collecting, hoarding, and saving." [9] The child's own feces are one of his first toys, and he does not hesitate to play with the contents of his diaper. The child is weaned from this "toy" through deterrents and threats of punishment. The child still enjoys playing with and manipulating moist street mud, collecting it in large heaps and making pies. Ferenczi says that this heap of mud is already in a sense a symbol, distinguished from the real thing by its absence of smell, and thus is for the child deodorized *dejecta*.

As the child's sense of cleanliness increases, through the help of pedagogic measures, he rejects mud and avoids "dirty things" that may soil his body or clothing. The symbol of filth must undergo a further distortion, dehydration. The child then plays with sand for hours, which his parents sanction, for such playing is "healthy" and "hygienic." However, the "return of the repressed" takes place, and the child fills the holes he digs in the sand with water, boys often employing their own urine for this irrigation.

Next in the progress of cleanliness is the stone age: the collecting of pebbles, which, like mud and sand, are gathered from the earth. Next are glass marbles, buttons, fruit pips, and the like. These can be used for barter or money exchange; and the child decidedly enjoys the collecting in itself. Soon stones begin to wound the child's feeling of cleanliness. He longs for something purer, and this is offered him in shining pieces of money. The high appreciation is in part due to the respect in which they are held by adults, as well as to the possibilities of obtaining through the coins everything that the heart can desire. At first, however, it is not these purely practical considerations that are operative, but enjoyment in the playful collecting, heaping up, and gazing at the shining metal pieces. The coins are treasured less for their economic value than as pleasure-giving objects.

Although Ferenczi's description of the steps in the development of the child's interest in money may seem quite speculative, psychoanalytic research has demonstrated with clinical evidence the probability of these relationships. A patient reported a special way of making copper coins shine. He swallowed them, then searched his feces until he found them, and, during the passage through the alimentary canal, they had become shiny. And there is the tired old joke in which the doctor, by means of a laxative, helps a child expel a piece of money that the child had swallowed; the doctor is told he may keep the piece of money as his fee.

The delight in gold and the possession of money may represent a symbolic replacement and a reaction against activity and hidden memories from the stage of toilet training in childhood. In other words, Ferenczi, Freud and other like-minded colleagues have emphasized that possession of money as an end in itself probably has its origin in infantile development.[2, 9, 11, 15] In acquiring bowel control during toilet training, the child is confronted with two simultaneous sets of social modalities, holding on and letting go. If "to hold" is retained as one's life pattern, then he may be dominated by the trait "to have and to hold." Thus, gold becomes a symbolic replacement for excrement, and one's character traits become the reverse of his childish pleasure in activity during his period of toilet training.

Jones states that the character traits that may develop out of the toilet stage of psychosocial development are extremely varied, owing to the complexity of the child's relationships with parents, nurse, and siblings, as well as cultural and socioeconomic factors interacting in the home.[15] Some of man's firmest qualities are derived from this complex: individualism, determination and persistence, the love of order and power of organization, reliability and thoroughness, generosity, the bent toward art and good taste, the capacity for unusual tenderness, and the general ability to deal with concrete objects of the material world. Some of the unhappy qualities are irritability and bad temper, hypochondriasis, miserliness, pettiness, proneness to bore, a bent for dictating and tyrannizing, and obstinacy.

During the stage of development in which the child exhibits a predominant interest in his excretory functions, he also manifests reactions of cruelty toward the people in his environment. That these two tendencies coexist in the same stage of development may explain, in part, why cupidity is associated with cruelty in man's mind. Shakespeare dramatized the two traits in Shylock. The possession of money arouses contradictory reactions: admiration and envy, hatred and disgust.

Possibly many factors other than those considered by Freud and his colleagues enter into the development of the so-called anal character. One may assume that, aside from constitutional factors, the character of the parents and especially that of the mother is important. The mother who insists on strict toilet training and who shows an undue interest in the child's processes of evacuation is usually a woman with a compulsive, rigid character structure who often lacks joy in life. Her anxiety contributes toward making the child afraid of life and attracted to rituals and objects that bind his anxiety. In other words, the toilet training as such does not lead to the formation of an anal character, but rather the character of the mother who, by her rigidities and fear of life, directs attention to the process of evacuation and in other ways molds the child's energies toward a pattern of possessing and hoarding.

The basic psychoanalytic theory discussed here can be criticized for neglecting the cultural, economic and political factors that must be considered today for an understanding of the psychological implications of money.[4, 14, 20] Also, one may disagree sharply with the deterministic and materialistic interpretations of personality development as expounded by Freud, Ferenczi and Jones. Their ideas and pioneering work, however, cannot be ignored in any discussion of the psychology of money. In other sections of this book, vivid testimony is given to the constellation of factors that enter into the development of a particular type of human behavior. Heraclitus' words, written centuries ago, should help us keep our efforts at behavioral interpretation in proper perspective: "You cannot find the boundaries of the soul, even if you travel every road; so deep is the measure of it."

CONCLUSION

Two questions frequently asked regarding the psychological meaning of money are: *1.* To what extent do attitudes toward money represent timeless traits of human nature? *2.* To what extent are attitudes toward money influenced by social and personality types that vary with the culture, institutional setting, and class situation?

It is generally believed today, from research and clinical observation, that the factors in the two questions are relevant in some degree in every person, and that they overlap. The personality traits that make for various attitudes toward money depend in part on social influences on the child, through the family and other community forces, during the years of personality formation. Thus one finds thrifty, generous, greedy and hoarding people in most societies, but the frequency distribution of and the valuation given to these traits vary greatly.

"Abnormal behavior in money matters and in other economic situations is often due to a conscious or unconscious clash of conflicting value systems in the mind of an individual." [18] Although abnormal economic behavior of the individual develops out of specific individual experiences, especially those of early childhood, we must consider two additional factors in order to arrive at a reasonable analysis.

The first concerns the cultural value scale and the socioeconomic setting that classify a given behavior pattern as abnormal, while another culture or society might view it highly favorably. The second factor concerns the comparative incidence, in various phases and strata of society, of different kinds of personality and behavior. For example, there have been many more misers in some societies than in others. They were considered normal and socially useful in seventeenth-century Geneva, while they are regarded with disdain in contemporary America. A long depression may, however, reverse this negative view about misers. Sopkins's *Money Talks* reveals a common denominator among the group of millionaires studied.[25] All of the millionaires were touched, in one way or another, by the depression of the 'thirties, and the fear of another depression seems a driving force in their lives.

In our affluent country, where the possession and earning of money have become for many the chief goal in life, Thoreau reminds us of an ancient truth: "Money is not required to buy one necessity of the soul." The humorous but sobering words of a wealthy patient to his psychiatrist echo the same sentiment: "By the time I discovered that money did not buy happiness, I already had five million dollars. What do I do now, and where do I go from here?"

REFERENCES CHAPTER 1

1. Abraham, Karl: Contributions to the theory of the anal character, *in* Selected Papers, London, Hogarth, 1948.
2. ———: The spending of money in anxiety states, *in* Selected Papers on Psychoanalysis, London, Hogarth, 1927.
3. Amar, Andre: Essai psychanalytique sur l'argent, Rev Franc Psychoanal *20*:322-344, 1956.
4. Brown, Norman O.: Life Against Death—The Psychoanalytical Meaning of History, New York, Knopf, 1959.
5. Desmonde, William H.: Magic, Myth and Money. The Origin of Money in Religious Ritual, New York, Free Press, 1962.
6. Erikson, Erik H.: Identity and the Life Cycle, New York, Internat Univ Press, 1959.
7. Feldman, Sandor S.: Contributions to the interpretation of a typical dream: finding money, Psychiat Quart *26*:663-667, 1952.
8. Fenichel, Otto: The drive to amass wealth, *in* Collected Papers, Series Two, New York, Norton, 1954.
9. Ferenczi, Sandor: The ontogenesis of the interest in money, *in* First Contributions to Psychoanalysis, translated by Ernest Jones, London, Hogarth, 1952, pp. 319-331.
10. Fingert, Hyman M.: Comments on the psychoanalytic significance of the fee, Bull Menninger Clin *16*:98-104, 1952.
11. Freud, Sigmund: Character and anal erotism, *in* Collected Papers, translated by Joan Riviere, vol. 2, London, Hogarth, 1953, pp. 45-50.
12. Garma, Angel: On the pathogenesis of peptic ulcer, Int J Psychoanal *31*:53-72, 1950.
13. Gibran, Kahlil: The Prophet, New York, Knopf, 1923.
14. Gorer, Geoffrey: The American People, New York, Norton, 1948.

15. Jones, Ernest: Anal-erotic character traits, *in* Papers on Psychoanalysis, ed. 5, London, Bailliere, Tindall & Cox, 1950, pp. 413-437.

16. Keynes, John Maynard: Essays in Persuasion, New York, Harcourt, 1932.

17. Kingsley, Charles: Yeast, ed. 7, London, Macmillan, 1903.

18. Lauterbach, Albert: Man, Motives and Money. Psychological Frontiers of Economics, ed. 2, Ithaca (NY), Cornell Univ Press, 1959.

19. Loewenstein, Rudolph M.: Christians and Jews, A Psychoanalytic Study, New York, Internat Univ Press, 1951.

20. Pederson-Krag, G.: A psychoanalytic approach to mass production, Psychoanal Quart *20:*(#3)434-451, 1951.

21. Rado, Sandor: Fear of castration in women, *in* Psychoanalysis of Behavior, New York, Grune, 1956, pp. 83-120.

22. ———: The problem of melancholia and the psychoanalysis of pharmacothymia, *in* Psychoanalysis of Behavior, New York, Grune, 1958, pp. 47-80.

23. Richards, Audrey I.: Hunger and Work in a Savage Tribe, New York, Free Press, 1948.

24. Scherman, Harry: The Promises Men Live By, New York, Random House, 1938.

25. Sopkin, Charles: Money Talks, New York, Random House, 1964.

26. Spock, Benjamin: Baby and Child Care, New York, Pocket Books, 1957.

Uses and Misuses of Money

MONEY AND FAME brought to Somerset Maugham the freedom and privilege of pursuing a special goal, which, he said, was to master his craft. When critics accused him of writing for profit, he replied: "I found that money was like a sixth sense without which you could not make the most of the other five."

In seeking to understand the psychological uses and misuses of money, one should focus on the predominant money behavior of the individuals described. Such behavior must not be limited to that associated with neuroses, personality disorders or psychoses, nor can rigid psychiatric diagnostic categories be employed. For money behavior at a given time may be transient, situational and unrelated to deep-seated emotional problems.

COMPULSIVE SPENDING

Compulsive spending has little relationship to income, because compulsive spenders can never obtain all the money they need to spend. Some earn large salaries through hard work and spend everything they make. Others make less but incur debts in order to spend. Many resort to unethical and illegal activities to get the money they so badly "need."

The compulsive spender is comfortable emotionally only when he feels free to spend. Often he has no realistic need for the objects he buys or the services he contracts. Where one compulsive spender will spend simply for the sake of spending, another will spend compulsively for specific self-gratifying items. If a compulsive spender is forced to save some of his money, he may become emotionally upset until he can resume spending at will. In order to keep them solvent, accountants sometimes hide in a trust fund part of the income of compulsive spenders or place them on a rigid allowance.

Motivations for compulsive spending and the kinds of compulsive spenders are many. Although some of them are spendthrifts, no single motivation can encompass them. Some persons make a childish and exaggerated display of their wealth; spendthrift to the point of extravagance, they are driven by a compulsion to efface a sense of inferiority. Others feel an unconscious need to squander money in order to return to a passive-dependent status through self-inflicted poverty. As might be expected, some compulsive spenders maintain a reliable economic relationship with a member of their family or with a friend, who will come to their financial rescue when they overextend. Bergler writes:

The spendthrift basically represents a type identical with the miser except that, where the miser uses pseudo-aggression in the form of refusing money to others, the spendthrift applies a so-called "magical gesture." This gesture denotes an unconscious dramatization of the thought, "I will show you, bad mother and father, how I really wanted to be treated—with kindness and generosity." [1]

Bergler's comments are understandable in an analysis of those compulsive spenders who had neither money nor love in childhood. Their selfish spending in adulthood is an unconsciously determined means of giving themselves something akin to love. Unfortunately, in the process they often create debts, which their relatives have to repay. Spending behavior of this kind by a spouse can be a serious source of marital discord.

Histories of many compulsive spenders reveal that they come from the same family contexts that produce psychopaths and extractive personalities. Usually the father, cold and distant, relates to the child only as a disciplinarian, not with love. The mother often has many interests outside the home and feels guilty for neglecting the child and not spending more time personally in rearing him. She becomes overindulgent with material things, substituting lavish money gifts for love and affection. Another type of mother, who actually spends most of her time in the home with the same effect on the child, overindulges and overprotects him. What should be emphasized is that although the family constellations may differ, in all of them guilt, money substitutions for love, and overcompensations of some kind are operating. A typical pattern is that of one strict parent, usually the father, with the other compensating for his severity. The child's allowance is constantly augmented by the indulgent parent's secretly giving him additional sums. The child learns to spend all he has, for he is not long in discovering that an empty pocket is sure to bring him more money. Simultaneously, he can punish his parents for not loving him by creating parental anxiety about his rate of spending. The constant replenishment of spending money prevents him from learning the frustration of having to limit his purchases, to choose carefully between purchases, and to save for a future use.

For many compulsive spenders, charge-account buying is even more exciting than money. They equate the charge account with temporarily unlimited spending power. Their pleasure from spending exceeds the pleasure obtained from the items or services purchased.

Some meticulously honest compulsive spenders suffer as they undergo voluntary periods of great scrimping and saving until they have available the sum they need. Periodically, they go on spending binges and enjoy the sensual pleasure of being able to buy anything they want until their money runs out.

The behavior of compulsive spenders ranges from strictly honest to immoral and illegal. With glib tongues and charming personalities, some ingratiate themselves with others. Often, they borrow without intention of repaying, frequently victimizing the same person repeatedly. When blocked in this, they may fall back on sex appeal. To get the money they need they will either marry someone with money or become a mistress, prostitute or gigolo.

Some compulsive spenders work long and hard to earn the money they need. Others, finding routine work too slow a process, turn their immature, sadistic and extractive propensities to such criminal pursuits as gambling, blackmail, extortion, peddling dope, prostitution and robbery (after which they often beat their victims). As Wilde said of himself: These people can resist anything but temptation.

What does such behavior symbolize? Psychoanalytically, by symbolically attacking their parent surrogate and forcibly wresting from him the money they want, they obtain emotional gratification of their unconscious needs. While most of these individuals are labeled psychopathic personalities, in more than a few cases they are actually psychotic.

Some emotionally immature people earn excellent income only to give it all on payday to a parent or parent-surrogate, expecting in return to be taken care of in a manner symbolically equivalent to that of the passive-dependent child. Often they ask for and receive only a token sum of spending money. The parents pay all bills and may even require this grown child to spend most of his time at home, keeping them company. When he marries, usually after his parents die, he tries to continue the same type of relationship with his spouse. Such a person is willing to spend all to buy a facsimile of the emotional security of childhood. This attained, he is satisfied.

One wonders, also, about the individual who gives his check away on payday to a parent or parent-surrogate, whether he is giving it out of fear or to protect against misfortune. Aesop's fable of a lion, donkey and fox who formed a partnership and went hunting illustrates an action in a relationship motivated by fear. When these animals had taken a quantity of game, the lion told the donkey to share it. The donkey divided it into three equal parts and bade the lion choose one. The lion leaped on him and in a fury devoured him. Then the lion told the fox to divide the game. The fox placed nearly all of it into one pile, leaving only a few morsels in the other. He told the lion to make his choice. The lion then asked who taught him to share things in that way. He answered, "What happened to the donkey?" Thus the fox shared out of fear of attack and injury, illustrating the dynamics of some parent-child relationships.

Narcissistic compulsive spenders—the show-off, the competitive, and the affection-buyers—should be of special interest to fund-raising agencies. The *show-off* spender must have a large audience, for he enjoys astonishing people by the lavishness or unusualness of his spending; he enjoys giving money only to those institutions and organizations that will give him the publicity he craves. The *competitive* spender retains his social prestige by outspending others in his social group. The *affection-buyer* tries to buy love from almost any source to bolster his feelings of inferiority; his efforts are mostly self-defeating, however, because he often befriends immature individuals, or backs unworthy and ill-conceived causes. Instead of the affection he craves, he gets ever insistent demands for larger handouts. Other narcissistic spenders disburse their money lavishly for clothes, jewelry, beauty treatments, and plastic surgery. Their all-consuming goal in life is to enhance their appearance and thereby to attract the admiration of others.

The self-pitying individual spends money compulsively only when he is mildly depressed. At such a time, he may feel no one loves him. By showering gifts on himself he may help his spirits improve. After a quarrel with her husband, a wife may spend money freely on clothes for herself. With the purchases, her anger at her husband subsides. Kaufman relates that several patients during hospitalization for surgical procedures secretly sent themselves flowers, fruits and other gifts, with effusive get-well wishes written and directed by themselves.[8]

Bargain hunters and suckers for easy money are both compulsive spenders and nonspenders. (We do not refer to those who seek bargains legitimately, in order to stretch a limited budget.) They buy things they don't need because they are cheap. Consciously, they persuade themselves that they are saving money; unconsciously, they may be leading themselves to the poorhouse. For them, bargain windows have the excitement of a battlefield. When they think they have outsmarted the seller, they have won that day's battle. They may have bought six stuffed alligators for the price of one, but a bargain is a bargain, and it is the *process* that is important.

In actual psychodynamics, the bargain hunter is treating the world as the perpetually refusing mother. To win in a bargain is not only to wrest symbolic affection from her but to wrest by one's wits more than she would ever give. Thus the bargain hunter is getting not only "love" but the better of a hostile mother—in the bargain.

Victims of flimflam artists are counterparts of bargain hunters. They will give over their life savings to almost total strangers for the lure of fabulous gain. Or they will invest their hard-earned money in enterprises about which they know nothing, with angelic confidence that their money so invested will bring them great security.

The motives behind the behavior of the sucker, of course, are complex. Their ineptitude and stupidity are obviously compulsive. What need is being served? Is it an attempt to find again the magical, feeding mother? Bergler contends that the unconscious motive operating in the sucker is psychic masochism.[1] This may be true sometimes, but to accept it as a general principle seems too much the idolatry of the unconscious mind. Under that postulation, the thing achieved is always what is willed. Such a concept is illogical, for it would seem to say "failure is really success."

The infantile spender literally throws money away. Chapter 3, "Childhood, Adolescence and Money," refers to the pleasure young children experience in seeing others scramble for the money they throw away. Certain alcoholics, senile persons, and psychotics get gratification from tossing their money away and watching the furor of others scrambling for it.

The compulsive spending habits of many people

have been a potent factor in the creation of professional financial advisors, who assume many roles in relation to their clients. These advisors, often Certified Public Accountants, begin as advisors and often end as father confessors. Their clients call them at all hours of the day or night and pour out their troubles in a kind of doctor-patient relationship. It has been said that the CPA is supplanting the psychoanalyst as America's newest status symbol, father image and subject for cocktail party conversation. This is not surprising, for today's value system considers holding on to one's money as important as holding on to one's sanity. Some of these financial advisors state that, left to their own devices, many of their clients would go broke in a boom.

COMPULSIVE NONSPENDING

Although the compulsive nonspender makes enough money to maintain a decent standard of living within his low, medium or high-income bracket, he has such a great fear of economic insecurity that his spending is inhibited. His unconscious fears push him to a minimal level of spending and a maximal rate of saving. This pattern continues despite large monetary reserves and no realistic basis for fear of economic insecurity. Such inhibited spending elicits descriptive terms as varied as conservative, economical, dollar stretcher, penny pincher and miser. The first three are defined in this manner by Kaufman:

The *conservative spender* is interested in getting his money's worth and no more, but limits his buying to necessities and few luxuries. The *economical* one is bargain-minded, spending much time and effort in finding goods and services he wants at the lowest prices. He is willing to sacrifice quality for price. The *dollar-stretcher* buys nothing that he can possibly make, and is constantly working during his free time to avoid spending either for finished products or services of others.[8]

The penny pincher, stingy person and tightwad are similar to the miser. Even if he possesses wealth, the penny pincher dreads having it known. He is obsessed by the fear of being robbed or envied, and becomes, compulsively secretive and miserly. The stingy person is self-punitive, depriving himself of things he needs or would enjoy even when adequate money is available for those things. The tightwad satisfies his physical needs by spending only when he must and mourns the loss of each dollar spent.

The miser subordinates everything to money, caring more for it than for the satisfaction of his physical needs. His compulsive accumulation of money is matched only by his obsessive thoughts about it. He gets supreme pleasure from physical contact with his money, his deposit slips, bankbooks and other symbols of a wealth whose existence he attempts to conceal from other people. He particularly worships inactive cash, which he may hide in his home; but at the same time, haunted by the fear of losing his money, he is unable fully to enjoy the impersonal power that money gives him. His constant excitement is expressed in indignation at the thought of being taken advantage of. He is also pathologically suspicious, always trying to outsmart imaginary enemies by refusing money and through pseudoaggressive acts reflecting cynical callousness.

The compulsive nonspender forms poor relationships with other people, probably because he unconsciously fears that they will deprive him of his money. The descending scale of warmth, scope and frequency of human contacts starts with the conservative spender and ends with the miser, who is often hermit-like. These love-hungry, money-hungry people, living by the principle that it is more blessed to receive than to give, get the reputation of being "spongers." Thus their interpersonal relationships lead to rejection; rejection reaffirms their belief that no one really cares for them; and this belief enhances their emotional isolation from other humans. Clinical studies reveal that some of these people in their early years were deprived of love, warmth and affection, and experienced instead poverty, punishment and regimentation. To them, money represents symbolically the love, affection and security that they never had but insatiably crave. They desperately need the insight of Kahlil Gibran in *Tears and Laughter:*

Money is like love; it kills slowly and painfully the one who withholds it, and it enlivens the other who turns it upon his fellow men.

Other clinical studies, however, show that some nonspenders did not suffer poverty, punishment or regimentation in their early years. Certain of the best-known compulsive nonspenders came from homes where no such conditions obtained. Disturbed relationships and deprivations at critical stages of development, not obvious enough to be noticed by the adult world, may nonetheless be sufficient to influence the child strongly. At some level of awareness, his behavior toward money relates to the basic human goal of getting and receiving love.

To help these people change the pattern of their money behavior is difficult. They feel that their approach to money is sanctioned by established social attitudes and that their "thrift" is a religious ideal. Kaufman emphasizes that often anything that forcibly dislocates a compulsive nonspending pattern may cause severe anxiety, panic, depression and many different kinds of psychosomatic illness, as well as a total breakdown in the person's capacity to adapt realistically to even minor economic reverses.[8]

At times, a person withdraws into miserly behavior because he has suffered financial injustices. George Eliot's *Silas Marner* illustrates such a situation. A little child, whom Marner adopted, led him out of his hermitage, restored his faith in normal human relationships, and helped him to accept a "proper" sense of values.

Most compulsive nonspenders are somewhat vulnerable to confidence men who promise them glibly the only form of love they can understand—an immediate, large increase in monetary reserves at small expense to themselves. When the swindle is revealed, the victims turn bitterly to an even lower level of spending.

In the lonely and disappointed, compulsive nonspending may occur as often as compulsive spending. An ever-present question for some is: "Since I am alone, who will look after me when I am sick or old?" This is a legitimate worry that, though it may lead to sensible saving, all too often leads the victim to deny himself decent living conditions. Not infrequently a news item tells the story of a ragged recluse who had hidden riches. In a squalid, self-constructed prison literally papered with money, such unfortunates live out their fear-determined lives.

GAMBLING

The Kefauver Senate hearings in 1950 and 1951 revealed that fifty million Americans participated in some form of organized gambling, and that profits accruing to gambling entrepreneurs were an estimated twenty *billion* dollars annually. The number of popular articles on compulsive gambling reflects the public's concern. The appearance and growth of Gamblers Anonymous, a nationwide organization to help problem gamblers end their habit, also attests to the widespread nature of compulsive gambling. Four hundred years ago, through his own addiction to all games from dice to chess, Cardano wrote well of the obsessional nature of the gambling disease:

> Even if gambling were altogether an evil, on account of the very large number of people who play, it would seem to be a natural evil. For that reason it ought to be discussed by a medical doctor like one of the incurable diseases.[11]

The compulsive gambler not only destroys his own resources; he is usually financially and emotionally costly to his family, friends, employers, and his community as well. A Cleveland salesman felt so guilty about his horse-betting losses that he took on an extra job, one for his family and one for his gambling. The motives behind gambling are also complex. Since those who gamble a great deal inevitably lose in the long run, one can say that a variety of motives are behind such compulsive urges to lose. Thus the winnings or the losses may be some kind of bonus added to the excitement of the gamble itself.

The decisive characteristic of gambling that differentiates it from other contests and speculations is the importance of chance in determining success or failure, the unpredictability of the results and the elements of risk and luck. Gambling is done by three different types of individuals: *a.* the normal person, who gambles for diversion and who can stop gambling when he pleases; *b.* the professional gambler, who chooses gambling as his means of earning a livelihood; and *c.* the neurotic gambler, who is driven by unconscious needs and is unable to stop gambling. Although these three types gamble for different reasons, conscious and unconscious, some of the same motivations are found in all of them.

Gambling seems to be a universally popular social institution. In our conventional society, monetary rewards are morally justified only as a result of hard work and thrift. Since easy money is considered ill-gotten, one can appreciate the immoral connotation associated with gambling. Gambling does enjoy in our culture, however, a marginal position as an acceptable social activity; it is connected, even, with religion. Many people have participated in church lotteries, and gambling has been described in primitive cultures where it is intimately tied up with religious rituals.[12]

Great literary artists have contributed to our knowledge of the unconscious motivations in gamblers. Dostoevsky's *The Gambler* portrays the character of such a person as a sadomasochistically ridden individual who is unable to break himself of this addiction.[4] Conrad's gambler is a homosexual with murderous hatred for women.[2]

Freud's contribution to the study of gambling is his brilliant essay on Dostoevsky.[5] On the basis of Dostoevsky's writings (especially his posthumous papers), his wife's diaries, and communications from Dostoevsky's personal friends, Freud formulated some of the basic concepts of gambling. During Dostoevsky's period in Germany, he was obsessed with the mania for gambling. He rationalized that he was trying by his winnings at the tables to make it possible for him to return to Russia without being arrested by his creditors. That this was only a pretext Dostoevsky was astute enough to recognize and honest enough to admit. His burden of guilt had taken a tangible shape as a burden of debt.

Dostoevsky knew that the chief thing was gambling for its own sake. "The main thing is the play itself," he writes in one of his letters. "I swear that greed for money has nothing to do with it, although Heaven knows I am sorely in need of money." He gambled until he had lost everything. Freud quotes from Fülöp-Miller and Eckstein: "He always remained at the gaming tables until he had lost everything and was totally ruined. It was only when the damage was quite complete that the demon at last retired from his soul and made way for the creative genius." [5] Repeatedly he gave his young wife his promise on his word of honor not to play any more on that particular day; he almost always broke his word. When his losses had reduced him and his wife to the direst need, he would then scold and humiliate himself before her, invite her to despise him and to feel sorry that she had married such a sinner. After he had thus unburdened his conscience, the whole business would begin again the next day. His young wife became accustomed to this cycle, for she had observed that the one thing that offered any real hope of salvation—his literary production—never went better than when they had lost everything and pawned their last possessions. Freud writes that when Dostoevsky's sense of guilt was satisfied by the punishments he inflicted on himself, his inhibitions became less severe and he allowed himelf to take a few steps on the way to success in his creative writing.[5]

Freud discusses how gambling is a substitute for, and derivative of, masturbation. The mania for gambling, with the unsuccessful struggle to break the habit and the opportunities it affords for self-punishment, is a repetition of the compulsion to masturbate. The emphasis on the exciting activity of the hands is the link that suggests the connection between gambling and masturbation. The irresistibility of the urge, the oft-repeated resolutions, the intoxicating quality of the pleasure and the heavy guilt feelings are present in both gambling and masturbation. Also, in both activities, Freud's studies lead him to postulate, there are unconscious fantasies of being rescued by mother or a mother figure. Many investigators disagree with Freud about the psychogenic connection between gambling and masturbation. The crucial point to remember, however, is the burden of guilt and the need for punishment. Dostoevsky's gambling was a good method of self-punishment. Thus it would not be rare to find in the analysis of a gambler that his motive was simply a more satisfying alternative to masturbation caused by childhood frustrations. At the same time, ample clinical evidence exists today to indicate that gambling may be an alternative to other sexual activity that has been frustrated.

The person with a gambling neurosis is one who must gamble, who cannot stop gambling, and who allows gambling to destroy or to tyrannize his life. Two decisive elements seem to be essential in the etiology of the gambling neurosis: *a.* the neurotic gambler feels lucky and hopes each time he will be rewarded, and *b.* he is impelled to test Luck or Fate. The normal and professional gamblers may have either of these qualities, but to a lesser degree.

The neurotic gambler hopes and, at times, believes he is lucky. Consciously or unconsciously, he feels that it is his right to ask Fate for special privileges and protection, and he hopes that Fate will prove that he is favored above all others by permitting him to win. Gambling is pleasurable not only for the money, but as a token of special privilege and power. The neurotic gambler seeks a sign from Fate that he is omnipotent, his longing for omnipotence, however, remaining full of doubts and contradictions. Thus, he gambles hour after hour, to convince himself that he is lucky (that is, omnipotent) and to gain occasional reassurance from Fate to calm his grave doubts.

The longing for omnipotence is generally believed to be carried over from early childhood—that time in the infant's life when all his needs were met instantly and he ruled everybody around him by crying. That power brought pleasant feelings to him.

Greenson, who has done a thorough psychoanalytic study of gambling, states that to the neurotic gambler, people are transformed into merely potential donors of narcissistic gratification, a characteristic of the orally oriented individual.[6] The gambling neurosis, like so many of the impulse neuroses such as the addictions and the perversions, is a defense mechanism against an impending severe depression. The neurotic gambler is an individual on the brink of a severe depression, and Greenson emphasizes that he deludes himself into feeling lucky and attempts to win a sign of favor from Fate that will gratify his urgent need for satisfaction and security. I strongly agree with Greenson's view of the neurotic gambler, as I have observed this clinically in a number of gamblers with severe depressive illness.

It was reported recently that a seventy-year-old woman was playing frantically two slot machines at a time in a Las Vagas gambling casino. While one machine was spinning, she was placing a coin in the other. The manager said the woman played every day for two or three hours. She seemed to introduce a frantic sense of urgency into the game. Whatever desire she was seeking to fulfill in her addiction, she seemed to be say-ing, "It is later than you think." Had this observer sought further, he would have found others, young and old, hoarding and playing at once as many as three slot machines.

Risk-taking is a part of the fabric of life, and bouts with chance often bring excitement in daily life or at the gaming tables. An old adage has it that a person is prouder of his luck than of his deserts.

Gambling can be seen as an adaptive phenomenon or life style. One individual may seek to eliminate as much risk-taking as possible from his life. Another may seek maximum risk in every activity, adopting the gambling approach as a way of life.

Some of mankind's greatest accomplishments have come about through the actions of men who were willing to take risks against the longest odds. Columbus took a chance that few men of his time would have taken in his search for a new route to India. Every investment today involves a risk and is something of a gamble. Bernard Baruch, in his autobiography, states that we would be foolish to try to stamp out the willingness in man to buck seemingly hopeless odds. He identifies our problem in money-making or governmental affairs as how to remain properly venturesome and experimental without making fools of ourselves. Unfortunately, as Baruch emphasizes, our emotions are constantly setting traps for our reasoning powers; and in the breast of every man there burns the urge to "beat the game" and show himself smarter than the other fellow.

The great financial genius, J. P. Morgan, insisted that he never gambled and even the use of the word in his presence regarding any financial venture elicited a negative response. Yet, one wonders if the word is not unnecessarily charged emotionally for many people. Sir

Ernest Cassell, the private banker to King Edward VII, is reputed to have said that when, as a young and unknown man, he began to be successful, he was referred to as a gambler. When his operations increased in scope and volume, he was known as a speculator. After the sphere of his activities continued to expand, he became known as a banker. Actually he had been involved in the same financial activities all along.

Obviously, no single motivation would encompass all gambling. The acquisition of unearned money, a form of greed, may be the least important of all motives, although the prevailing public opinion may be otherwise. A group of gamblers stated that the chief reasons for their gambling were intellectual exercise and inexplicable excitement.[18] They would not be expected to identify consciously such motives as the desire to prove one's superiority to the forces of chance, sexual compensation, or self-punishing tendencies. A prominent writer and lover of the gaming tables, whom I saw in Las Vegas, identified the chief motivation in gambling as adventure. He felt that all other motivations were secondary or derivatives of this chief one.

The crowds in casinos such as those in Las Vegas are fascinating to watch. A wide range of emotions is seen in their facial expressions: boredom, excitement, mania, depression, intense involvement, and business-like seriousness. In general, a sense of magic and enchantment pervades the atmosphere. One participant facetiously summed up his feelings about his favorite hotel and casino: "This place has all that mother could give and a lot more."

One who studies the gambler and his behavior is led repeatedly to a common denominator identified frequently in the pathological use of money. Addiction to gambling and the subsequent indebtedness of the individual seem to express a deep need for a close relationship to others, even though these "others" are glad to take his money. Such a need is another example of the isolation and alienation of man in his search for relationships of love and intimacy.

SPECIAL SITUATIONS IN THE USE OF MONEY

Denial of Economic Status. People deny their economic status through either pretended poverty or pretended wealth. Pretended poverty fends off enemies who may try to take their money. These "money deniers" distrust banks, often hiding their money in their homes or other secret places. Self-punitive and denying, they want to be pitied, to have a passive-dependent status. They gratefully accept handouts with attendant pity, but secretly relish the potential power of their growing, if hidden, monetary reserves.

Belief in the evil eye, not restricted to illiterate people, can be a strong factor in the denial of economic status. The evil eye is in essence a metaphor for envy. Successful and attractive people are, therefore, particularly vulnerable. Personal gains or advancements are often concealed. Among Mexican-Americans in south Texas, the evil eye is called *mal ojo*. They believe that some people are born with "strong vision," which can harmfully project admiration or desire of possession into a person or thing. Prosperous and healthy people naturally arouse envy and hostility. People with *mal ojo* have been known to project disease or misfortune on them by a mere glance. It is the malice, envy and hostility behind the glance that seem to cause the misfortune in the victim.

Deep in our tradition, of course, is the belief that the rich are in constant peril while the humble poor live in safety. This is illustrated by the ancient fable of the two mules that were traveling heavily laden, one with baskets full of money, the other with sacks crammed full of barley. The mule that carried the valuable load went along with his neck erect and his head in the air, shaking the bell on his collar to make it tingle loudly. His companion followed with a quiet, sedate step. Suddenly, bandits jumped out of a hiding place. In the murderous fight that followed, the first mule received a sword-thrust and the money was looted. The other mule was given no attention, for the thieves did not think the barley worth troubling about. The mule that had been robbed and wounded began to bewail his hard fate. "For my part," said the other mule, "I am glad they thought me beneath their notice, for I have lost nothing and I have a whole skin."

People who have lost their money often pretend to a wealth they no longer have. To attract rich people, perhaps with the idea of making "good" marriages, they spend lavishly of money they really should not waste. Their greatest problem, of course, is to maintain their front until their object is attained.

Charity and Guilt. Individuals give to charity for a number of reasons, some because they believe it is the duty of those who have money to share it with the needy or sick. The biblical record reminds us that from those to whom much is given, much is required. The story of the widow's mite measures the gift not by its intrinsic value but by the extent of sharing and by what is kept for oneself. Some give to gain the approval of others and to get publicity for themselves.

When the question is asked, "Why do people give?" one of the first replies is, to assuage their feelings of guilt. A person may consciously or unconsciously wish to make symbolic or actual restitution for some real or imagined antisocial act that he has committed; so he may give large sums of money to a charity, institution or individual. If he has evaded taxes, he may make an effort to pay them, or if he cannot do this, he may give to a worthy cause. He may give an anonymous gift or have his name associated with the gift or institution and no one may suspect his motivation. During periods of acute grief over the loss of a spouse or child, or some other member of the family, the grief-stricken person often gives money away for worthy and sometimes ill-advised causes. Feelings of guilt are a normal part of mourning, but if there is some actual or fantasied reason for feeling guilty after the loss of a loved one, the guilt will be even more intense and the need for expiation more critical. Fund raisers, and unfortunately exploiters, have learned this characteristic of human behavior and use the knowledge to obtain funds for their causes. Some religious groups, as well as private counselors, advise people to make no major decisions about significant donations to any cause until at least one or two years after the loss of a loved one.

A physician, speaking of his first years in medical practice, told of an elderly man whom he treated for tuberculosis. Although medically unnecessary, his children insisted that he see their father every day. This entailed driving forty miles round trip each day, but money was of no concern because oil had recently been discovered on the property. While the children were benefiting from the immense income, the father was not in a position to enjoy his new wealth, so this created an uneasy guilt in the children. Nothing, therefore, was to be spared in their father's medical treatment. The physician's daily visit to the father relieved the children's guilt feelings and, most likely, was also of some comfort to the father.

It is not uncommon for parents who lose a son in a

war to feel unable to spend the government life insurance left them. Some of them have said, "To spend this money for our own use would almost give the impression that we exchanged our son for money." The behavioral dynamics here are complex, but relate in part to their guilt over their inability to help and protect their child. Thus in their minds there is something "tarnished" or "unclean" about the insurance money; it is blood money.

The prostitute who gives the pimp large amounts of money may be doing so in part out of guilt feelings. She is giving away the "poisoned money" in exchange for his companionship. Possibly the pimp's taking the money brings a little relief by helping the prostitute feel that here is a person who is a little more degraded than she is.

Manipulative Uses of Money. Money is often used to manipulate causes as well as people. Such sayings as "The Almighty Dollar," "He who pays the piper calls the tune" and "Mary holds the purse strings" are descriptive of the power money can give.

Some philanthropic foundations refuse to give to certain schools or religious groups because they espouse "liberal causes," even though these "causes" may have only a peripheral or no relationship to the use that will be made of the money. Other foundations may use "loaded" gifts to encourage an institution to abandon a philosophy, position, or tradition of which they disapprove. Recently, certain philanthropic foundations have been under attack, and the Federal government has been urged to withdraw their tax-exempt status on the grounds that they were supporting political, social and religious issues to which the attackers were opposed.

Church members in the United States give more than

three billion dollars annually, pledges usually being made without regard to the minister's policies or convictions. Recently, however, some churches' strong commitment to civil rights has altered the picture, and their congregations have decreased sharply. Millions of dollars in pledges have been withdrawn in anger by some parishioners, while others have donated generously because they are in sympathy with this new Christian attitude.

Widespread publicity was given recently to remarks made by New York's Episcopal Bishop, Horace Donegan, at a ceremony marking his fifteenth year as head of the diocese. He announced that an irate parishioner had stricken from his will a pledge of six hundred thousand dollars toward completion of the Cathedral of St. John the Divine, and that two other wealthy benefactors were threatening to withdraw even larger bequests. The bishop said that his stand on civil rights—preaching prointegration sermons, sending priests to Selma, installing a Negro canon at the Cathedral, and integrating parishes—clearly accounted for this backsliding.

Other clergymen have experienced financial loss of support because of their position on controversial issues. The Reverend James Jones of Chicago, an Episcopal priest in charge of diocesan charities, was put in prison in 1965 for taking part in a civil rights demonstration. As a result, one layman rescinded a $750,000 pledge to the church's charitable agencies. Similar examples can be cited in churches across the nation.

This passion for selective giving is not new in the church. Throughout history, economic pressure has been put on clergymen who do not support the same causes as the "powers" in their congregations. These pillars of the church have expected their ministers to be spiritual vassals to them, not disturbing prophets and reformers. In their efforts to control their ministers and force them to accept their views, money, of course, has been the chief weapon. Happily, the coin has another side. Many attempts to silence the church through financial pressure have inspired sympathetic laymen to make up for lost pledges. This has been true in the South as well as in other areas of the country.

Loewenstein discusses the relationship of money to the repression and inhibition of physical force, in his psychoanalytic study of Christians and Jews.[9] In the formation of Jewish traits, historical development, social conditions, and childhood influences all converge toward a renunication of the use of physical force and violence. Repression and inhibition of physical force may lead to a fixation at either of two stages of psychosocial development—the oral or the anal. Arrest at the oral stage may be reinforced, in the case of the Jews, by attaching tremendous religious importance to the nature and preparation of food. This would account for the tendency to focus on food psychological conflicts arising from other sources.

On the other hand, much of Jewish psychology is not religious but cultural. Many psychological traits attributed to their religious traditions are derived from the people among whom they have lived. For instance, many of the traits of the Jews living in Russia and Poland originated in the surrounding Slavic cultures.[14]

Persons who have suffered humiliation often use money as a weapon of revenge and retribution. This is true both of those who already have money and of those who feverishly acquire money in order to even a score. How money operates for revenge or for retribution is fairly obvious. A recently published "Dear Abby" letter is a good example of revenge through the use of money [10]:

Dear Abby: Our son, who is married and living out of the city, has never given his father anything for Father's Day. Nor has he ever remembered me with so much as a card or a telephone call on Mother's Day. Our birthdays and anniversaries are ignored also.

We never fail to send him, his wife, and their children lovely gifts for all occasions. Knowing that friends and relatives would ask me what our son sent us for an occasion that called for a gift, I would buy something very costly and pass it off as a "gift" from our son.

He will pay for them in the end, however, because I have been keeping track of the cost, and instructions have been left in our will that after Dad and I are gone the cost of those items shall be deducted from whatever we leave. I thank you.

Money may also be used for manipulative purposes in handling one's rage. In a cartoon in the *Saturday Review*,* an elderly man says to his butler: "Harkness, get me my will. I feel like disinheriting somebody."

A prospective groom's ability to acquire money may of course be tested before marriage by the prospective bride, although the woman's testing is seldom appreciated by the man, who probably never forgets what seems to him a distortion of love. F. Scott Fitzgerald had such an experience. While Fitzgerald was working in New York as a copywriter for an advertising agency, to supplement his meager earnings from writing, the girl he loved refused to marry him. She implied that he was doing so poorly financially that maybe they had better call the whole thing off. Discouraged, he left his job and returned to his home in St. Paul to write a novel—*This Side of Paradise*, which he sold immediately to a publisher with an advance of $5,000. Then the girl consented to marry him. The marriage was off to a bad start. Fitzgerald wrote in his diary that after

* January 30, 1965.

this he was never the same. The fact that his girl had turned him down because he didn't have any money gave him an abiding distrust of the wealthy. Also he never forgave Zelda Sayer for refusing at first to marry him, and for the rest of his life he blamed his failures and his bad luck on her. Out of the way he felt about Zelda, and out of his relationship with her, came the central situation of his most famous novel, *The Great Gatsby*.

Ritual and Fetishistic Uses of Money. Kaufman has seen people in his medical practice who are impelled to count their money repeatedly in times of stress. When the crisis is acceptably passed, they no longer have the compulsion to count their money.[8]

A particular coin or sum of money may be used as a good-luck charm, the individual's self-reliance and peace of mind being contingent on his having this monetary fetish always with him. Young people often wear a coin stuck in the leather strap of their loafers as a kind of good-luck piece. It may also be worn around the neck, arm or leg for the same purpose. Others find it a psychic mandate to carry with them a large sum of money. This is often done to avoid a possible recurrence of a previously embarrassing situation.

The biblical story of the lost coin (Luke 15: 8-9) illustrates the ritualistic and symbolic meaning of ten pieces of silver. On her wedding day, a woman received ten drachmas from her bridegroom, which were used for ornamentation. Upon losing one of the coins, the woman was distressed until she found it. In ancient times, the number ten was used as the number of perfection, and represented fidelity and the integrity of the marital partners. Thus, the woman's lost coin symbolized a temporary breach of the marriage bond.

A professor at a theological seminary told a story

about his serving as visiting pastor of a church one summer. After service one Sunday, a man asked him what he thought of a particular theologian at the professor's seminary. This colleague, although world famous, was known to arouse controversy because of his theologically unorthodox views. The professor spoke with enthusiasm and devotion for his colleague. The man was obviously displeased with the favorable comments and said little, but that evening the professor found that someone had dropped a little package containing thirty pieces of silver through the mail chute of his home. It was later learned that this man was in the habit of giving such a gift quietly and secretly to anyone who he felt had betrayed Christ.

Human life is filled with ritual. As in ancient times, modern man's involvement with superstitious ritual is prevalent in many areas. Ritualist acts are not genuinely instrumental acts, being compulsive and not purposeful. Performed from need, they are best interpreted as expressive behavior, since they help a person control his inner anxieties. They make sense too when regarded as symbolic representations rather than practical measures. It is natural that money should find a place in our superstitions, since our word comes from *superstitio,* which implies not only religious dread but "standing over a thing in amazement or awe." We can readily see then how with objects such as money, superstitious practices are still in existence while their significant connections have long since disappeared.

Use of Money by Psychotics. The first indication of a breakdown in the reality function of an individual may be his inappropriate uses of money. The paranoid schizophrenic may spend money in a manner that indicates he thinks someone may be overcharging or robbing him. He may hide money in his clothing and shoes, and since he fears that any display of his buying power may lead to attacks from powerful imaginary enemies, he greatly restricts his spending.

Other schizophrenic individuals exhibit odd or violent behavior in their use of money. They may have no recollection of what they did with their money, and may appear indifferent to the consequences of their spending. They may buy an expensive object and adore it, or purchase a piece of junk and enjoy it just as much. They may attack and rob a stranger, or give money to a person whom they later will assault and kill. Their spending behavior is chaotic and unpredictable. Many schizophrenics, during remission of their symptoms, try to maintain a passive-dependent relationship to some person whose advice about money matters they try to follow. In this way, they are saved from pathological uses of money.

The manic person is erratic in his spending. His interest jumps from one thing to another; even before one deal is consummated he may be already involved in a different money transaction. His spending orgies are often accompanied by sexual promiscuity, heavy eating and drinking. During the manic phase of his psychosis, a man may launch a successful business project only to dissipate his resources. He often has legal difficulties, because his income and spending are usually not in equilibrium. Some of the most interesting case histories in psychiatry describe the eccentric buying and spending patterns of manic individuals, for when they have great resources at their disposal, the unbelievable often happens.

The president of a family-owned business suffered periodically from a manic phase of his psychosis. His activities during these phases became a subject of gossip in the community. At one time, he gave a large party and had the band members play most of the evening while standing waist-deep in the water of his indoor swimming pool. The people he employed seldom hesitated to carry out any antics he suggested, because he always paid them handsomely. At another party he gave in his home, a new piano was found to be out of tune, so he had it thrown on the trash heap and ordered another to replace it immediately.

The depressed person may spend little or nothing, yet become more depressed with his every expenditure. As his depression is setting in, he may guiltily use some of his money to make symbolic restitution for his real or fantasied antisocial acts. As his depression deepens, he finds he is unable to continue working and earning. He feels impoverished, unworthy and unloved, and may be unable to eat or sleep, thus making his condition even worse.

Use of Money by Students and Trainees. Many students have to struggle so hard to raise the money to pay their college expenses that the strenuous effort leaves a materialistic mark on them. If they incur a fairly heavy debt during their training period, the struggle to repay this may continue for years. An excellent example of this is the physician. In medical schools, scholarships are few, and tuition and other fees are high. After the four years he devotes to studying for his MD degree, the physician spends one year in an internship and three to five years in a residency. Unless he is reasonably solvent, he borrows money and finally enters practice owing, possibly, several thousand dollars. By this time he may be married and have children. After renting an office, purchasing the equipment he needs, and hiring an assistant or two, he is so far in debt that he is overwhelmingly concerned with making money to meet his obligations. He is almost too insistent on collecting an adequate fee from every patient he treats. After seemingly endless years of trying to pay his debts, and to give his family the comforts they were denied during his training, it is almost impossible for him to avoid developing a materialistic viewpoint. Even after his financial condition improves, his materialistic visions have become so crystallized that his preoccupation with money often continues.

The same thing is true of students in many other professions and trades. Thus failure to provide financial assistance for higher education contributes enormously to the materialism of our society.

EXTRACTIVE BEHAVIOR

Among the individuals who use extractive behavior in their interpersonal relationships, none are better known than "the success hunter," "the dependent one," the "hustler," "the imposter and embezzler," and "the swindler." Although students of human behavior such as Bergler [1] identify the motivation behind the conduct of this group as being psychic masochism, this term is not an adequate dynamic explanation. The goal of this group seems more the normal one of getting and receiving love and achieving intimacy in human relationships. A study of their behavior, however, reveals the problem of "conflict of interest" in human affairs, and the repetitious and often destructive or self-destructive patterns of conduct between people. The goal of achieving love and closeness in human relationships thus becomes distorted.

The capacity of these extractive individuals to defraud others could hardly be more cogently illustrated than by the following case. The parents of a boy referred their son for psychotherapy because of his seemingly unlimited capacity for extractive behavior. His ability to charm or cheat others out of their possessions was unbelievably subtle and effective. Later, an argument arose between the psychiatrist and the parents. The parents paid willingly all the bills for psychotherapy, but they absolutely refused to pay the thousand dollar loan their son had managed to borrow from the forewarned psychiatrist.

The Success Hunter. The "success hunter" has contempt for moderate earnings. He has high ambitions and entertains exaggerated ideas of success. In the pursuit of his goals, he is ready to work hard but experiences a constant inner tension. When he lacks new excitement in business and the opportunity to exhibit himself, he feels dissatisfied and suffers from boredom. He is hypersensitive, cynical, overly suspicious, opinionated, and contemptuous of the unsuccessful person, whom he treats in a ruthless manner. Although on the surface it may seem out of character for this type of person, he nevertheless suffers from a great many doubts that his luck may not continue. He is harassed by hidden depressions, hypochondriacal worries, impotency, and the inability to enjoy the simple pleasures of life.

The Dependent One. The "dependent one," having maneuvered himself into a position of dependence on another person, complains bitterly of the disappointments that the inconsiderate stinginess of the provider is causing him. When dependency needs are totally frustrated, great rage is mobilized against the former provider who, of course, never asked to be appointed to the position in the first place.

Not all dependent personalities are full-time parasites; some work sporadically. During low-income periods, however, they fall back again on friends and acquaintances for help. Once again, money being insufficiently forthcoming, their lament begins. Such individuals remain naively unaware that human benevolence is a two-way street. Although in common with us they are seeking a relationship of love and intimacy, they remain blind that such relationships thrive on reciprocity—on giving as well as receiving. Their orientation, however, being directed toward the neurotic need to receive, they persist in their delusion that the world owes them a living.

Hustlers. Money without work is the platform of these emotional cripples, their commodity being good looks and sex appeal. Sex, however, through which they lure their victims, really holds little excitement for them. Money is their goal. Cold and often violent toward victims who compensate them inadequately, hustlers often attach themselves to partners who treat them even more cruelly than they treated their victims.

Imposters and Embezzlers. In general, "imposters and embezzlers" are narcissists who through the development of skillful social techniques and the display of charming and disarming manners, inspire confidence and friendship. Often witty and gay on the surface, they are frequently suffering from buried depressions and are privately cynical and seemingly remorseless in their attitude toward others.

Although as "confidence men" they succeed in "conning" vast sums from the unsuspecting, thereby gratifying their driving need to inspire love and admiration, they cannot long enjoy their ill-gotten gains. It is characteristic that they must reveal themselves and take their punishment. The psychodynamics of such people, according to Bergler, evolve out of oral disappointment with the mother, coupled with helplessness to take revenge on her.[1] But they can victimize society, and that is their revenge—a short-lived revenge as it proves, for apparently only the unconscious anticipation and acceptance of punishment makes crime possible for such persons. The harsh punishment imposed by society appeases their conscience and is actually what they are seeking.

Motivations for embezzling by the bank teller or other trusted workers in business and industry may be quite different from those of the so-called professional embezzler.* The users of intrusted funds or property generally have an unusual economic need, and they may be ashamed to ask anyone to help solve it. Such embezzlers have the problem of overcoming their conscience. They accomplish this by rationalizing that they are only borrowing the money or property and will return it. The unusual economic need may be related to gambling, extravagant living standards, unusual family expense, inadequate income, undesirable associates, improvident investments, mental irresponsibility, and revenge, as well as numerous other factors.

The Swindler. Closely related to the group already described is the swindler. He is discussed separately because of his special relationship to the victim in his extractive behavior. The swindler can be viewed as a player, for his mode of existence is playful, and his motivations lie in the sphere of sport. Swindling, a playing form of crime, is connected with personal achievement, with the desire for honor and fame. The swindler always has to gain the victory over his victim; when he proves himself more clever than his victim, he feels that he has done himself credit.

Some swindlers show so strong a need to prove themselves superior that they frequently boast of their vic-

* Norman Jaspan and Hillel Black, in *The Thief in the White Collar*, tell the revealing story of America's billion-dollar-a-year embezzling business by trusted employees.

tims' stupidity. Others persist in their fraudulent actions out of a bitter need. Many are emotional cripples,
particularly in interpersonal relationships. Swindling
and sexual abnormalities are frequently seen in the
same individual. Certain swindlers are attracted by the
adventure of putting one's whole existence at stake and
thereby mastering a difficult situation, as well as conquering fear. In our land of law and order there are not
many opportunities for wanderers or adventurers, or
even for escape from one's self. Zeegers emphasizes this
point: "Swindling, that play of imagination, is still left
as a playground for those who are unfit to play their
parts in society or who are tired of being what they
are." [15]

In a game of swindling, two parties are necessary.
The swindler usually detects in his victim a sense of
larceny, a susceptibility to flattery, an openness to
dubious affairs, and a hunger for prestige or fame. The
victim readily believes what the swindler tells him because it coincides precisely with his own inner desires.
Thus the swindler in a sense succeeds in "reading the
mind" of his victim and correctly interpreting his
wishes. Studies of the swindler and his victim reveal
the presence of similar unconscious tendencies within
both: the wish for unlimited bounty and the feeling of
personal infallibility.[15]

Although in a context different from that of the usual
swindler and his victim, the wish for unlimited bounty
and the feeling of personal infallibility could nowhere
be more beautifully illustrated than in *Life*'s report
(April 7, 1967) of the Medderses and the Poor Sisters.
One day Ernest Medders, a $200-a-month employee of
an oil distributor, heard that a Mississippi lawyer was
filing a lawsuit in behalf of some 3,000 clients who believed that they owned a share of a Texas oil field

worth about $500 million. He and some of his relatives were among the eligible plaintiffs. Medders soon began to believe not only that the suit would be won, but that he would be the sole heir and would receive the entire $500 million all by himself. This conviction his wife shared, and she spread the word of their soon-to-be-gained affluence at St. Joseph's Hospital, where she worked as a practical nurse. St. Joseph's Hospital is operated by the Roman Catholic teaching and nursing order whose official name is the Poor Sisters of St. Francis Seraph of the Perpetual Adoration, Inc. The nuns, seemingly seeing a new and generous benefactor in the Medderses, began to lend them money to help press the claim. At first the loans were small, but gradually they increased to as much as $60,000 a month. The Medderses moved from Memphis to Muenster, Texas, and established a ranch there. In five exciting years the Medderses ran through nearly three million dollars in a spending spree that fooled and shocked both the nuns and the state of Texas. Many of the socially prominent and rich people they entertained lavishly found the sham almost impossible to comprehend. The financial joyride began its downhill course when the Poor Sisters acquired a new mother superior, one of whose first acts was to stop the loans. Actually much earlier the US Supreme Court had thrown out the suit involving the rich oil field.

Texas came in for further publicity when art swindlers duped Dallas multimillionaire Algur Hurtle Meadows. Meadows had always been considered a tough man at the bargaining table. Evidently he was no match for the manicured art swindlers who had the means and authority to impress him. He found himself owning probably the largest private collection of fake paintings in the world, for which he had paid hundreds of thousands of dollars. His bargaining skill was used, for example, to secure a painting for $45,000 instead of the $100,000 selling price. If such paintings as that one had not been fakes, Meadows would indeed have had cause to rejoice. In spite of his recent ill luck in art, he feels that the world remains a kindly enough place, where a young man has only to venture out, keep his word, know his trade, trust in others, heed the advice of his seniors, and bargain for the best terms.

CONCLUSION

In Aristophanes' *The Clouds* (423 BC), there is a splendid scene in which a troubled individual consults the philosopher, Socrates. The patient, Strepsiades, is told to lie on the couch, to think and speak freely, and thereby to reach understanding of his problems. Unfortunately, Strepsiades does not know precisely what his problems are, except that he is tense and anxious and does not sleep well. Socrates directs him simply to say anything that comes into his mind. Strepsiades begins to talk, of all things, about the moon. Socrates encourages him to go ahead and talk about the moon if he wants to. Through a series of free associations, Strepsiades builds the fantasy that if he could only capture the moon and put it in his pocket, his financial problems might be solved. While in his pocket the moon would not wax and wane. Thus, the first of the month could be prevented from making its appearance and Strepsiades would not have any debts to pay. His symptoms and wishful thinking are strangely reminiscent of the money-sickness that plagues modern man.

The proper use of money gives the individual a sense of well-being and emotional security. Inappropriate uses of money may create, as well as grow out of, deep emotional conflicts. Money-sickness is one of our most common illnesses but often not recognized as such, by the individual involved or by others. Nonetheless many psychosomatic complaints grow out of "money-sickness" and find their way to the psychiatrist because many people feel much too self-conscious to discuss money woes with their family physicians.

Often people are as secretive about their money as Victorian ladies were about their sexuality. The Jourard and Lasakow researches in self-disclosure reveal that information about one's money situation is a topic disclosed to others *in very low degree*.[7] My own experience with patients bears that out. They show far less resistance in relating hatred for their parents or in disclosing sexual perversities than in discussing their money status or transactions. It is as if they equated money with their inmost being.*

Many are alarmed by the widespread preoccupation with material things today. Ernest Dichter has pointed out that the public's shift away from its puritan complex is enhancing the power of three major sales appeals: desire for comfort, desire for luxury, desire for prestige. In his publication *Motivations*, he states:

We now are confronted with the problem of permitting the average American to feel moral even when he is flirting, even when he is spending, even when he is not saving, even when he is taking two vacations a year and buying a second or third car. One of the basic problems of this prosperity, then, is to give people the sanction and justification to enjoy it and to demonstrate that the hedonistic approach to life is a moral, not an immoral, one. This permission given to the

---

* An old proverb of India indicates that secretiveness regarding money matters has been with us for a long time: "Never make known one's wealth, one's remedies, one's lover, where one has hidden money, the good works one does, the insults one has received, or the debts one has contracted."

consumer to enjoy his life freely, the demonstration that he is right in surrounding himself with products that enrich his life and give him pleasure, must be one of the central themes of every advertising display and sales promotion plan.[3]

The advertising industry and professionals such as Dr. Dichter, who serve the industry, fail to recognize the crucial issue that possessions are meant to serve life, but that life comes first. Most of us cannot help feeling a little embarrassed over the biblical reminder that "a man's life does not consist in the abundance of his possessions" (Luke 12:15). The abundance of our worldly goods seems to be creating a threat to the quality of our lives. Our economy is partly based on our becoming quickly dissatisfied with last year's models, and we are so firmly fixed on the treadmill of production and consumption that it is difficult to step aside and tell where this process is leading us. Reinhold Niebuhr calls our attention to the dilemma of achieving "a measure of grace" in an economy of abundance, and points out that we are in danger of developing a culture that is enslaved to its productive process, thus reversing the normal relation of production and consumption.

Today, money seldom symbolizes a tradition of love, service and unity, although it is often used to overcome isolation and lack of closeness in human relationships.

REFERENCES CHAPTER 2

1. Bergler, Edmund: Money and Emotional Conflicts, Garden City (NY), Doubleday, 1951.
2. Conrad, Joseph: Victory, London, Methuen Ltd., 1924.
3. Dichter, Ernest: Motivations, April, 1956.
4. Dostoevsky, Fyodor: The Gambler, New York, Macmillan, 1931.
5. Freud, Sigmund: Dostoevsky and parricide, in Strachey,

James, ed.: Collected Papers, vol. 5, London, Hogarth, 1953, pp. 222-242.

6. Greenson, Ralph R.: On gambling, *in* The Yearbook of Psychoanalysis, vol. 4, New York, Internat Univ Press, 1948, pp. 110-123.

7. Jourard, Sidney M.: The Transparent Self, Princeton (NJ), Van Nostrand, 1964.

8. Kaufman, William: Some emotional uses of money, Acta Psychother *1*:20-41, 1956.

9. Loewenstein, Rudolph H.: Christians and Jews, A Psychoanalytic Study, New York, Internat Univ Press, 1951.

10. New York Journal-American, June 25, 1964.

11. Ore, Oystein: Cardano: The Gambling Scholar, translated by S. H. Gould, Princeton, Princeton Univ Press, 1953.

12. Stocking, Collis: Gambling, *in* Encyclopedia of the Social Sciences, vol. 6, New York, Macmillan, 1931, pp. 555-558.

13. Wykes, Alan: The Complete Illustrated Guide to Gambling, Garden City (NY), Doubleday, 1964.

14. Zborowksi, Mark, and Herzog, Elizabeth: Life Is With People, New York, Internat Univ Press, 1955.

15. Zeegers, Machiel: The swindler as a player, *in* Slovenko, Ralph, and Knight, James A., eds.: Motivations in Play, Games, and Sports, Springfield (Ill), Thomas, 1967.

Childhood, Adolescence and Money

IT IS THE RESPONSIBILITY of any good parent not only to give good advice but to set a good example regarding the meaning and handling of money. As in all areas of child behavior, the best counsel and a fine example are no guarantee of how a boy or girl will turn out. One of the challenging problems for both child and adult is to see how well he can match his income and his expenditures. The following discussion of the practical aspects of money incorporates suggestions for helping the child mature with a solid appreciation of the value of money and other human resources. It is to be expected that many things about money will confuse the child, even in his early years. He will be further confused when he discovers that money is often used as a measure of personal worth. Thus, the growing child's adjustments to money and money concepts will be numerous and often painful.

Most studies have shown that a child's notions about money are usually vague until he reaches his fifth year. William Kaufman has pointed out that the child's first emotional satisfaction regarding money comes from literally throwing money away.[6] His first acquaintance with money may come accidentally as he secretly explores his mother's pocketbook and finds a small hoard of coins and paper money. He examines the money, plays with it, then stuffs some of it into his mouth but quickly decides he doesn't like its taste. He spits out the money and throws the rest away. Often his older playmates or strangers scramble for it. The sight amuses him.

Kaufman goes on to discuss the meaning of money for children. His findings are gathered from his busy medical practice and have the ring of authenticity. From ages three to five the child learns to pass coins to salespeople under the direction of a parent. He gradually realizes that by giving money to the right person at the right time and in the right place, he can get things much more desirable than the money. At this stage, the child believes that money has magical properties. His parents obviously can, by putting their hands in the right pockets, draw on what seems to be an inexhaustible store of money and buy with it anything they want.

From ages five to nine, the child learns to manipulate the coins of various denominations at his disposal. At this stage, he develops some of his most important emotional reactions to the symbolic meaning of money and money transactions. He learns about purchasing reward foods such as candy and ice cream. He then learns about obtaining toys and comic books with money, and how money can be used to gain admission to the circus or the movies.

Shortly after a child discovers that money can buy exciting things, he begins to ask for some money of his own to spend as he wishes. Children learn rather quickly parental attitudes toward money and its importance, or lack of importance, in various aspects of life. Most parents find it difficult to educate their children objectively in the use of money and question how much and how often money should be given the child. The traditional view is that money must be *earned* before it can be spent. Many parents take this view seriously out of fear that their children might get the idea that money comes easily and is not to be taken seriously. Parents, however, cannot stick to the "earning before spending" principle, because children need money of their own long before it is possible for them to earn it.

Even during these early years of the child's life, money becomes associated in his mind with pleasures. Parents use money not infrequently as a reward to re-enforce habit development of various desirable forms of behavior. At this time the child makes the connection between love and money.

ALLOWANCES

Skill and wisdom regarding money come to children largely by managing money of their own. The weekly allowance furnishes the child the means for practicing the art of making choices and using his judgment about what to spend his money on, how much to spend, and how to save for spending next week or next month. Many parents are reluctant to give a child money of his own because he may squander it on the playground or elsewhere for worthless things or may even lose it. Fortunately, most parents remember that allowances are actually not for buying valuable possessions but for buying valuable lessons.

Pearson is right in stressing that a child should learn some of the unpleasant aspects of reality with money.[10] He advocates perfect freedom in the child's use of his allowance, with the understanding, of course, that the allowance is adequate for his age, sex, and social situation, and once it is all spent there is no more money forthcoming until the next allowance day. Such a procedure teaches him the reality related to the value and concept of money. It is almost impossible for him to learn this if the parents inform him how he should spend it or insist on controlling his expenditures. Of course, the child may seek counsel at times, after he has made bad purchases, been cheated, lost his money, or made unwise decisions. After such experiences, parents have special opportunities for teaching and guidance in money matters. At other times, the child is simply allowed to profit from an experience, either good or bad. For example, it is considered good for the adolescent girl to be allowed to select her own clothes, within the proper price range. If she selects unwisely and has to live with the results of her choice, she will be more sensible next time, as she will have only herself to blame.

The child learns to manage money as he learns other arts and skills—by practicing with the tools and materials. Practice in the management of money can come *only* with money of his own, because in this way he learns when to spend and when to hold back, how to choose among many possible buys, and how to save for something better. Many parents have reported that their relationship with their children improved when the boys and girls were put on an allowance and no longer had to coax or beg for money.

Many parents resist giving a child an allowance. They can give the child anything but money. In this, parents show their own need to retain coins and paper money that they have worked hard to earn without possibly ever getting enough to satisfy all of their needs or wishes.

If a child's allowance is started early, money wisdom will be slowly acquired and accompanying mistakes relatively inexpensive. When his money experience starts with nickels, dimes, and quarters, hopefully he will be wise when the time comes for him to handle dollars.

Parents should show a businesslike and responsible attitude toward the child's allowance. The allowance should be given as a regular routine on the same day each week, whether the child has been polite and helpful or rude and lazy. Some of the educational value of the allowance is lost when the child has to ask for his money each time or when parents hand it over reluctantly or as an indulgence.

Child specialists discourage withholding a child's allowance as a disciplinary measure. Such a practice, like the payment of a reward for good behavior, strengthens the child's tendency to think of money in terms of love and to feel that he is disliked if money is withheld from him. The allowance is an educational tool, a way of letting children learn about money. How can a child manage his money affairs if his income is suddenly cut from seventy-five cents to fifty cents? Such punishment may imply to the child that friendliness and responsibility are worth only twenty-five cents a week. The child must learn also that there is no price on such qualities as politeness and responsibility. They cannot be bought for money or paid for when lacking. The question of money must not enter where it does not belong.

A child, age five or six, is ready to receive an allowance. In the early years, when the sums involved are relatively small, the child's age carries more weight than the parent's income in deciding the size of the allowance. Many parents raise allowances as soon as the child seems to show any judgment about using his money.

The increased allowance may not mean that the parents are spending more money on the child, but rather giving him a chance to do more of the choosing and spending himself. Of course, what the allowance is expected to cover should be the most important factor in determining its size. If ice cream, candy and toys are all that will be purchased, the six-year old may need the same allowance as the ten-year old. However, if the ten-year old is expected to pay for milk at school, bus fares and club dues, his weekly church pledge, and the equipment he needs for his hobbies, then he may need several dollars. Gruenberg focuses clearly on the issue: "Parents want to be very clear in their own minds (and thus help their children to be clear) as to what part of the allowance permits choice in spending and what part permits none." [3]

Parents and children understand one another when they both recognize the difference between earmarked money and spending money. As the child gets older, his learning to manage earmarked sums is more important for his maturation than having expense money doled out to him daily.

Allowances are to be adjusted from time to time as the child's needs and interests change. He will want and need the experience of managing more money as he gets older. For example, as a girl matures, her allowance can gradually be adjusted to include items of clothing, beginning with simple things and going on to larger purchases. Thus, during her high school years she will be making most of the decisions about what she spends for clothing as well as for entertainment. A boy becomes interested in clothing a year or two later than a girl, so clothes will not become an item in his allowance until his early teens. Since boys are often allowed to go out alone before girls are, the "entertainment" item may appear in a boy's allowance before it is included in a girl's of the same age.

Boys and girls need practical suggestions from parents about carrying money safely, keeping track of

money, keeping accounts, reasonable borrowing, unwise borrowing, and saving.

SAVING

The savings bank suggests to the young child "Think
of tomorrow" at a time when only today matters. Saving does not have much meaning to the small child, for
he does not value money. As he gets practice in shop-
ping and choosing and learns the marketplace value of
different sizes of coins, he will probably of his own
accord, when he wants something special, wait a few
weeks until he has saved up the sum he needs. Thus
saving for a purpose, to purchase something or to do a
particular thing, is the best way for a child to begin
saving. Gruenberg warns, in *The Parents' Guide to
Everyday Problems of Boys and Girls:*

Saving is not a habit that can be forced upon an individual. It is a way of thinking and feeling. Part of the process
of growing up is learning to plan for the future. It is natural
for children to live for today and let tomorrow take care of
itself. Only gradually are they able to measure time in
longer and longer spans. A five-year old can hardly imagine
tomorrow, let alone next week. But at nine the same child
can begin planning in October the presents he will give for
Christmas.[4]

Although forcing a child to save is rarely effective,
the child can be helped to stick to his purpose and thus
make saving a satisfying experience instead of a dis-
agreeable one. At times the parent can help the child so
plan his spending that some money is left to save for
the summer trip with his school class. It also seems
appropriate for a parent to help the child when a realistic financial goal cannot be quite reached. Also the
child can be given spontaneously a little financial boost
from a parent. The child can use an occasional boost to

keep up his resolution, when saving with a particular goal in mind, for example, to buy a bicycle or to go to camp. Also the child must be guarded against attempting the impossible, for this would be dangerous to the spirit as well as to the savings program.

Most child specialists feel that when a child, either of his own accord or through his parents' efforts, makes too great a point of saving and is unable to spend and enjoy spending, his attitude toward money is less wholesome than that of the youngster who cannot save at all. The child who must hoard and accumulate money for its own sake is usually unhappy and anxious, seeking in this way a sense of security. When such a tendency is not strong, the parents can help the child by discussing with him the real purposes of saving and spending. When the tendency is marked, so that it is painful for the child to spend and seemingly necessary for him to hold on to his money, parents can be certain that the child is in some kind of emotional trouble and that the hoarding is a symptom of it. They may be able to find the difficulty by sympathetically watching for the cause of his insecurity. Probably they will need the help of a child specialist who knows about the usual troubles of boys and girls in growing up.

Parents should remember that a child who spends freely is more easily guided than one who holds on to his money. The child who is timid and hesitant about spending his money, even for purchases that he really wants, can be encouraged by discussing his purchases with his parents and having them go along with him the first few times when he wants to buy things.

THE CHILD'S WORLD OF REALITY REGARDING MONEY

The child's assessment of reality regarding money can lead to many misinterpretations, often setting the stage for future difficulties in money matters. When a parent sticks to a fixed allowance and refuses to give additional money, a youngster may shout: "You don't love me any more!" At this point, the child still believes that his parents have an unlimited amount of money, which is being withheld from him for parental reasons. Depending on the parents' handling of the situation, the child can make either a good or bad adjustment to the initial shock of not having as much money as he wants. When the child learns his monetary limitations, he must make for himself the choice of whether to save or spend. His management of this crisis now will determine much of his attitude about money as an adult. He may, for example, learn relatively early to increase his income by running errands or doing little jobs for people. Or, conversely, he may learn to extract money from his parents by nagging them or by becoming a professional nuisance, in other words, mastering early the art of soliciting bribes.

As the child's social life develops, he discovers that some children have more money than he has. Envy raises its head. Others he meets have less money than he has. Envy of the rich gives place to a sense of superiority over the poor. Significantly, the child's already formed feelings about money will determine whether he prefers playing with children who have more or less money than he has. In his future relations, will he always react to people in terms of their economic status?

Gradually, a child's ideas of "mine and thine" become more sharply differentiated, but a small child has a hard time distinguishing between them. The young child may take an article that does not belong to him. He says that it is his for the simple reason that he wants to use it at the moment. This desire for possession lasts only as long as his interest in it. How soon he learns the lesson of right of private property will depend on what he sees and hears in his own family. Members of some families are very casual in their use of one another's clothing or playthings. In other families, to touch anyone else's objects means war.

Children should learn the difference between what is theirs and what is not as early as possible. Parents err in letting a child take other people's things because he is "cute." The right of private property is the way of the world. The sooner this is learned the less friction there will be for the child and others in his environment.

The child should be given a place to keep his things, and other members of the family should respect his possessions. If a visitor comes he should be encouraged, not forced, to share his playthings with him. If he does not want to give up one toy, another should be found for his visitor. Very early a child may learn to exchange what he has on a this-for-that basis, or even to try to buy love and friendship by giving his money or his toys to others in his play group.

Imbuing a sense of responsibility is vital. Children need to learn early how to work, how going without a lesser object may gain a greater object. They need the maturing influence of regular chores fitted to their age and development, and to be encouraged in developing new work projects. There should be a part for the child in the work and play programs of every home. "Spare the 'work load' and spoil the child" is no idle cliché. A work program in the home is easy to institute but difficult to enforce. Each member of the family, including the parents, must do his regular job without nagging or coercion. Applegate writes: "A hall blackboard in which reminders, messages, and plans can be written

will save much harmful bickering and can be the
source of many family chuckles—the best kind of noise
any family can make." [1]

There are many viewpoints regarding children and
work. Dr. Roy R. Grinker, of the Institute of Psychosomatic and Psychiatric Research, Michael Reese Medical Center, Chicago, in studying mentally healthy
young males found that one of the things they had in
common was *an early work history*. Laziness in children is usually caused by lack of interest or poor
health. The healthy child cannot stand being idle; he
has to be doing something all day. Children from age
three to eight will work hard without thought of reward in most any type of activity such as carting sand
or bricks. They identify themselves with adults, and
their work is like a fantasy instead of reality. For the
age group nine to twenty, dull manual labor is very
burdensome. This age group, however, will work end-
lessly on old cars, radios, bicycles, and similar objects
of great interest to them.

As the child becomes increasingly aware of the desir-
ability of material possessions, he may wonder why his
parents cannot have as many wonderful things as the
parents of his friends. Here unfolds further the fundamental, if traumatic, truth—his parents are not omnipotent; there is a limit to their buying power. This realization may create strong feelings of anxiety and anger
in the growing child. Since the father is usually the
chief wage earner, the child's anger may be directed
chiefly against him. Kaufman reports that children in
such a situation may kick, bite or punch the father, and
that "parents usually do not recognize the cause of the
child's anger, anxiety, mild depression, rage, temper
tantrums, deep insecurity feelings, and other psychosomatic illness." [6]

In evaluating a child psychologically, I often ask him what, should he be granted any three wishes, would he wish for. It is surprising that occasionally a wealthy child wishes for a grocery store so that his family will always have plenty of food. Obviously, the parents have painted a bleak financial picture to this child. What he needs is reassurance and love, and to be taught gradually that there is sufficient money to take care of his basic needs and even some for luxuries. He should be helped to realize that there is no real cause for worry, since he will be well taken care of by loving parents.

Actually, as soon as a child is old enough to understand, he should be initiated into the mysterious workings of the family budget. Then he knows firsthand why he and the rest of the family have to take turns in getting the things they want. In order to avoid giving the neighbors undue "entertainment," the size of the budget need not be mentioned.

Inevitably, a child will make an unfavorable economic comparison between his father and a neighbor. Enraged, the father may retaliate by becoming harsh and punitive toward his child. He may criticize everything the child does with his money, to the extent that the child becomes an anxious and frightened user of money. Here a parent's unconscious anxieties about money and economic security are brought to the surface—the child becoming the scapegoat. If this behavior continues, it may engender abnormal attitudes toward money in children, which may affect them the rest of their lives.

The emotionally insecure child of five to nine, and even an older child, may try to solve his conflicts about money in one of several ways. He may become subservient to richer children, hoping for monetary favors, or may fight to take what he wants from them, incidentally punishing them for being richer than he. He may, on the other hand, select only playmates who have less money. With them his sense of inferiority is assuaged. He may withdraw completely from the harsh world of money into a fantasy dream world where the great wealth of imaginary relatives would give him unlimited, if make-believe, buying power. Or, he may decently try to earn money to supplement the parental allowance.

If there is poverty in the child's family, he may experience real physical privation. This may affect his feelings about himself and others, for to be hungry and cold is to feel unloved and insecure. Real physical deprivation, resulting from the lack of money, may cause the child to view money as a tremendous source of power for the gratification of needs and wants. The shock for him is great when he encounters schoolmates from affluent families, which have plenty of money for luxuries while he has none for necessities. Poverty may handicap him in making meaningful relationships outside his family. He may feel that he is different, that he can't compete, and that he doesn't count.

There are also special emotional strains that affect children in families of wealth. Often parental ambition presses for achievement beyond the interest and capacity of the child. Emphasis on money and social position, material competition with the neighbors (keeping up with the Joneses), the actual deification of money as an evidence of superiority—all these attitudes penetrate and distort the minds of children. Where in such synthetic atmospheres can true values be instilled into children?

The child learns early in life that money can be earned. He seeks to supplement his allowance by doing jobs of one kind or another, especially for neighbors. Also, there are often opportunities for earning money in one's own family through "jobs" around the house. Gruenberg writes that "something can legitimately be called a job if *a*. parents might otherwise hire somebody else to do it or *b*. the boy or girl has the right to refuse it." [3] The child, then, does not get paid for something he has to do for his share in day-to-day family life—such as tidying up his room, helping with the dishes, or going to the grocery store. He gets paid for chores one might otherwise hire somebody else to do, such as mowing the lawn or washing windows. And he has a free choice whether or not he will accept the job offer. The wages should be agreed on in advance by parent and child.

When jobs are not available around the home, parents often help older children to find suitable outside employment. Sometimes this is advisable even when employment possibilities exist at home, the relationship to an outside employer being less emotional than the parent-child relationship.

When a child begins to earn a significant amount of money, parents often wonder whether he should be allowed to keep it all. If the parents do not need the money, they usually like their children to have some extras out of the income they are earning and to put some of it aside for future use. If the family really needs part of the money, then the situation ought to be explained thoroughly to the child and his consent obtained. A child's understanding of his parents' financial condition increases as he himself begins to earn money. At this stage in his development, he can be told more about the family financial picture. Then parents and youngster, together, can decide what part of his own expenses he may now be able to take on.

As boys and girls get older, they can be included more and more in their parents' discussions about money. The children will learn that almost daily there are decisions to be made about money, sometimes large and sometimes small.

Earning money is a valuable experience for the child. A wise man once declared that he would give anybody a dollar who would give his child the chance to earn a quarter. A child usually learns the value of money when he works for it. A sense of responsibility on the job, self-confidence, self-discipline, and learning to get along with other people are valuable benefits derived from working on a job outside the home.

A prerequisite to happiness is the conviction of one's own worth and dignity. The individual's sense of worth receives major nourishment from work and the rewards that it brings. The parent's own sense of worth and of being rewarded for his labor is reflected in his parental ability to develop in his children trust in the future and convictions about the worthwhileness of work. Children, from their earliest years, are exposed to such pressures as "do your best," "get ahead" and "measure up." Our society communicates to the child that effort is rewarded, and that success follows if he tries hard enough. Implicit in this philosophy is the corollary idea that failure to succeed is somehow the child's own fault.

Belief in this concept of success is of major importance to the family in which the father's earnings are not sufficiently high to meet the family's needs adequately. Although economic history and economic reality have established the fallaciousness of the idea that failure is the penalty of shiftlessness and unworthiness, this belief is still held by many in this country and finds its target in the individual who fails to make money.

STEALING AND MONEY CRIMES BY CHILDREN

The child of five or six has a fairly clear idea of personal property, and understands that he is not to take things that belong to others. Most children, however, even at seven or eight, occasionally come home with some object that has been filched. When the parent discovers his child in a theft, the child should not be drastically punished or humiliated, because at this age he does not know the difference between right and wrong in the abstract. The need for his parents' affection and approval is his strongest motive for doing what is right. He needs to understand that what he has done is wrong, but he also needs the assurance that his parents love him and will help him to do what is right. When parents help the child return the stolen object or make necessary restitution, the child is reassured that he still belongs to those who are good and lovable and that he is not doomed to be a thief.

A child of school age rarely steals just to possess an article. Occasionally he keeps on stealing because he has learned that his wants are easily satisfied without his being caught. Usually there is a much deeper reason, the need to satisfy some inner drive. The motivations for stealing are complex and can be evaluated only by a study of the individual. Some children steal because of the symbolic meaning of the object. When trying to discover why a child steals, it may be found that motivation is rather simple or straightforward. For example: a boy may be under pressure to contribute to a school cause; since he cannot get the money from his parents, he steals. He may steal to spite someone who has been abusing him. He may steal in order to have the same things his friends have if he can get them no other way. He may steal to gain the approval of a gang or other peer group.

In studying teenagers who have been caught shoplifting, one often discovers that initiation into a club may require a prospective member to steal a specified amount and type of goods. Thus the problem of status and the need to be accepted often play decisive roles in these situations. The motivation may even be unselfish, to help out at home. The child who steals is often having trouble making friends, and erroneously attempts to buy popularity by appearing affluent.

Josselyn has pointed out some of the symbolic meanings of stealing. She stresses that stealing an object may represent stealing love, of which the child feels deprived. A little girl may steal something from a boy, but symbolically she is stealing his penis. A little boy may steal from his mother with magical expectations that thereby he will deprive her of her power over him. In some cases, he will steal to deprive her of the baby growing inside her, who, he fears, will replace him.[5]

A child may also steal to invite punishment when he needs punishment for some hidden reason. A classic example of punishment-seeking is the child whose face is smeared with jam from the forbidden container. Why didn't he wash his face and avoid being caught? The child may take something or behave in some other unacceptable manner to test parental response or gain parental support. He may take money from his mother's purse even though he knows his mother is aware of the amount she has. Such acts may represent the wish to be punished in order to strengthen his own disapproval. This pattern of behavior is usually a transient one, but if it persists, the underlying problems may be more significant than they appear at first.

Children may steal because of the need for adventure. In rural areas they may steal watermelons from a neighbor's field or apples from his orchard. City or suburban life gives children little opportunity for such excitement or adventure without imposing a penalty. The urban child may pick up things from a store, which are often not wanted, the adventure being gratifying in itself. "I did it for kicks" is the reply often given by children who have been caught stealing. Snatching a piece of merchandise and dashing for cover has pleasing elements of danger, and of rebellion against authority. It is often not the act but the circumstances under which it is committed that make the difference between youthful mischief and juvenile delinquency. This type of stealing is often done in groups, or its excitement relived in telling about it to the group. Although this behavior should be controlled and not condoned, its seriousness should not be overrated. Often the child sees the act in better perspective than his parents do. In order to neutralize stealing as a form of excitement, parents should provide the child with wholesome experiences of novelty and adventure. Many youngsters have found their need for excitement satisfied in recreation centers, youth clubs, camping, and scouting.

Kaufman writes of the alarming tendency in youngsters under the age of nine, and influenced by radio, television, movies and comic books, to solve their basic money conflicts by entering into criminal activities of both amateur and professional caliber.[6] He cites instances of how these amateurs rob other children, deliberately short-change people they run errands for, or effect minor shoplifting in stores. Some have planned and successfully executed complex and daring robberies, even opened safes, in order to get money they felt they needed and which their parents were unwilling or unable to give them. Consistent with Kaufman's observation is the report that in a large Southern community the director of a boys detention home noted that the crime rate for robbing parking meters rose steadily from zero after such an incident appeared in a daily comic strip.

Ralph S. Banay, President of the Medical Correctional Association and a professor of forensic psychiatry, reports that a generation ago prisons and reformatories were the only graduate schools in the techniques of crime, but today this curriculum has been extended and brought into every home through mass production of films of violence for television. He stresses that many crimes committed in real life by young people today prove to be repetitions of acts they "committed" in fantasy while watching television.[11]

THE ADOLESCENT AND MONEY

The solutions for the adolescent's money problems are mostly variants of those described for younger children. If the adolescent has developed constructive solutions to his money problems earlier in childhood, he faces his contemporary adolescent money problems with good reality function and formulates workable plans for his future education and employment.

The tumultuous adolescent stage, which is marked by a conflict between dependence and strivings for independence, presents special problems in relation to money. Since the adolescent is in large measure dependent on his parents and yet desires to assert his growing independence, there is a reactivation of his earlier anger against his parents for not being able to give him all the money he thinks he needs.

The adolescent in school has sharply increased expenses for social and personal obligations. As his increased need of money is a part of his sexual awakening, he spends much of the money available to him to enhance his attractiveness to the opposite sex. Growing into adolescence, he becomes increasingly aware of economic class distinctions. He experiences anxiety about his future as he is confronted with the necessity of planning for his education, his career, and marriage. He needs support, control, and also freedom of choice. His normal conflict about independence and dependence can most readily be expressed through money.

Feldman has summarized the adolescent's problems with his family concerning money matters: "The adolescent is likely to express part of his healthy rebellion against his family by a strong reaction against *all* family patterns, including family patterns of thrift and expenditure. He uses money as a way of measuring his parents' standards and behavior and as a way of depreciating them." [2] He may be critical of their economic failures or deny the importance of their successes. He may even criticize them on ethical grounds, or flout them by adopting a conflicting political ideology.

Inconsistencies and ambivalences manifest themselves frequently in the adolescent's use of money. He may be alternately stingy and wildly spendthrift. He may be resentful that parents place no control on his spending, and particularly angry with them if he makes a poor purchase. At the same time, he wants to buy what pleases him and often spends his money defiantly. Great flexibility on the part of parents is required if the adolescent is to be given some freedom and yet be provided with some controls. Parents must approve sensible use of money but not be too critical of errors in spending.

If parents exercise too much restraint over the adolescent's spending, he may capitulate and never free himself from parental controls, because at this period his ambivalence is great and he fears the loss of his parents' love. On the other hand, he may become so rebellious that he never learns to manage money adequately. In the adolescent's demands for money, he may be expressing a frustrated need for love. The problem of dependence-independence, and his alternating movements into one or the other of these phases, can overshadow the adolescent's fear of the loss of parental love, and drive him to the reckless use of money.

Often, parents are reluctant to see their child grow up and emancipate himself from them. They know that when the child grows up, he grows away from them. Money offers many opportunities for defensive behavior on the part of the parents who rationalize that the child will squander his money. Parents may act out their own feelings about money through a child. If they were deprived of money in their childhood, a not uncommon response is to permit the adolescent to use money in whatever way he wishes.

Most adolescents have parents around the age of forty. This age is a period of inventory-taking for parents. The father, whose masculine status is threatened by his son, may attempt to set up rigid controls, at the same time accusing the mother of overindulgence. The mother, threatened by her daughter's attractiveness, may try to compete with her by controlling her selection of clothes or curtailing money for cosmetics. She, in turn, will accuse the father of overindulging the daughter. Such family rivalries are normal unless they stem from deep-rooted and unresolved conflicts in the parents.

Frances Feldman wisely counsels that parents should endeavor to stand together on major decisions about the adolescent's use of money.[2] On many of the minor issues, however, they should permit each other to guide the adolescent of their own sex, so that the boy can identify with his father and the girl with her mother.

Parents ask why children in a particular family often have totally different attitudes toward money. One sibling may be a spendthrift and another a hoarder. This is a complex matter relating to one's life experience, influences at critical stages of development, and constitutional endowment. In other words, the child's money behavior represents a subtle blend of nature and nurture. A factor often overlooked is that parents never treat two children exactly alike, for parents change almost daily in response to an array of experiences and stresses. One father asked why his older daughter threw money away and his younger daughter was quite close in her spending. This difference in behavior could probably not be adequately explained by a single determinant; yet, one could speculate that there were significant differences in the handling of these children during critical stages of their rearing.

During adolescence, children begin to develop many interests outside the family and to think seriously about their careers. Those who carry financial burdens in families with limited income usually encounter greater problems in becoming emancipated than those in more favorable circumstances. On the other hand, out of despair or frustration, they may escape from the family abruptly and prematurely and, since they are breaking away under unfriendly circumstances, carry with them a residue of emotional dependence and hostility.

At times, during a financial crisis, as during the great Depression of the 'thirties, an adolescent is forced to give up his adolescence and become a major wage earner for the family. This necessity may deprive the adolescent of his basic emotional needs, and distortions of personality may result. One of these distortions relates to his use of money. Often his tendency to altruism or sharing will be blunted, and he will have a tendency to hoard. On the other hand, such a person may become overly generous with his own children and quite helpful to others in need. In general, though, the old maxim holds that "a starving man cannot share his food." The conditioning that took place during his period of deprivation will never let him forget his previous hunger.

Fortunately, the adolescent who has had reasonably secure and satisfying experiences through these emotionally charged years can be expected to respond realistically, as an adult, to his financial responsibilities and opportunities.

Many parents have become alarmed by the influence of present-day advertising on children, especially teenagers. Their alarm would increase if they read such books as Vance Packard's *The Waste Makers*[9] and *Hidden Persuaders*,[8] and Martha W. Lear's *The Child Worshipers*.[7] Advertising agencies have teen-age sections for developing special advertising techniques to meet the challenge. Credit cards are being pushed by many stores across the land. Some stores advertise that parental approval is not necessary in order to open a junior charge account. An official of the National Retail Merchants Association exhorted department stores to open up junior charge accounts, because teen-agers offer a "made-to-order opportunity for the sales-minded credit executive." Packard points out this bit of alarming hypocrisy: "The stores inviting Junior's patronage on a credit basis usually profess to be utterly uninterested in him as a customer. They just want to help him become a more prudent citizen by offering him an educational program in money management."[9]

The Council on Consumer Information commented on some of the plans that stores were making for teenagers by asking: "Are they attempting to follow the biblical admonition—'Train up a child in the way he should go and when he is old he will not depart from it'?" Packard reports that the president of New York's Bowery Savings Bank said that teaching the young to spend on credit is tantamount to teaching them to use narcotics.

This marketing approach with teen-agers is a far cry from the sign hanging in a store of former days: "Minors must have permission from parents before they can spend over two dollars."

Thus, the marketplace is introducing new dimensions and a variety of complications regarding money into the lives of adolescents and their parents. The teen-agers have been identified as having big wants, big allowances, and often their own earned, big-sized spending money.

Aimed at children and teen-agers, advertising is looked on by outraged observers as "the insidious manipulation of young minds." Advertisers have learned that the buying patterns of parents can often be influenced or even controlled by a child. Even when the television commercial is not directed to the child, advertisers can depend on him to hear and to spread the word. Sitting attentively before the TV set, the child, first to know of new products, acts as a product information bureau in the home. The American parents' addiction to pleasing the child is a factor on which advertising agencies capitalize heavily.

This preoccupation with consumption and other forms of materialism appears to be having a heavy impact on the attitudes of young people being reared in the new environment. Some investigators are reporting findings that do not match the traditional conception of American youth as ambitious, dedicated, self-sufficient idealists who hope to build a better world. A recent study of eighteen hundred youths in ten countries, conducted by Harvard University psychologists, revealed that American youths were more self-centered and materialistic in their aspirations than the youths of most of the countries surveyed.[9] The youths in the study were asked to visualize their future. A conspicuous finding was the preoccupation of American youths with the material aspects of their existence to the exclusion of most other concerns. They knew specifically the kind of rich, full life they wanted to build and could identify the material possessions they wanted to bring the fulfillment.

Students of various countries were asked: "If you should get a large sum of money five years from now, what would you do with it?" Only two percent of the Americans thought of sharing such a windfall with anyone beyond their immediate families; the impulse to share with other people in need was higher in virtually every other national group. Of course, one can take strong issue with this study. Many American youths are insulated from those in need, but when exposed to the needy they share as generously as any other national group. Materialism and the pursuit of wealth do not necessarily deaden sensitivity to other human beings. American philanthropy, our programs of social change, and a multitude of youth projects attest to this.

CONCLUSION

Parents often ask about the key factors or influences during childhood that enter into the formation of adult attitudes toward money. They are not always easy to identify. One parent asked if he could be given a code or a kind of "ten commandments" to use for inculcating in his children sound attitudes toward the uses of money. Suggestions or hints are available for this parent, but hardly a set of commandments:

1. The child should be given experience in managing some money of his own.

2. He should be taught the relationship of money to work and encouraged to earn money through part-time jobs.

3. Parents should set good examples in the use of money and try to give good advice.

4. Responsibility regarding property rights should be developed in the child.

5. Security, both economic and psychological, must be experienced by the child in his social and family setting. The child should not be made overanxious about financial matters. If most of a family's energy, realistically or unrealistically, centers around warding off starvation, love of life is stunted.

6. Justice must prevail, in the sense that one child should not be made to feel inferior to another. In the community, if one social class of children exploits another and prevents the other from sharing in the unfolding of a rich and dignified life, then the children of both classes will suffer from distorted values.

7. Consumer training, given by parents and school teachers, should be an essential and continuing part of the growing child's educational experience.

8. Parents' attitudes about money, and the way they treat things of value that represent the expenditure of money, create lasting impressions on children; therefore, neither cavalier disregard nor undue reverence for money is desirable.

9. Parents should be flexible and try not to expect more of a child than he is capable of handling, because each child matures at his own rate of development, and possesses his own individual approach to money.

10. Although teaching the child to save his money for

future needs is desirable, learning to buy wisely can be just as important.

Parents should not use money as a reward for good behavior, good grades, or personal services. Avoiding the use of money as a reward also avoids crossing that sensitive line which divides a *reward* from a *bribe*. The child must not be guided into a philosophy that doing his best is necessary only when hard cash is to be gained. Parents should avoid using money as an instrument of authority and domination over their children. Children in such a family will not learn much about sound money management, but will learn only that one must kowtow to tyrants.

It is obvious that all relationships in a family are influenced by the inescapable psycho-socio-economic demands of a money world. The child's experience during his formative years, the economic and social position of his family, the attitudes and feelings of the family about money and social status, the way money is handled with the child—these will inevitably affect his attitudes as he emerges into an adult world with adult responsibilities.

REFERENCES CHAPTER 3

1. Applegate, Maurie: Everybody's Business—Our Children, Evanston (Ill), Row, Peterson, 1952.
2. Feldman, Frances Lomas: The Family in a Money World, New York, Family Service Ass of America, 1957.
3. Gruenberg, Sidonie Matsner: Money of their own, *in* The Encyclopedia of Child Care and Guidance, Garden City (NY), Doubleday, 1954, pp. 935-944.
4. ———: The Parents' Guide to Everyday Problems of Boys and Girls, New York, Random House, 1958, pp. 319-346.
5. Josselyn, Irene M.: The Happy Child, New York, Random House, 1955.

6. Kaufman, William: Some emotional uses of money, Acta Psychother (Basel) *4:*(#1)20-41, 1956.

7. Lear, Martha W.: The Child Worshipers, New York, Crown Pub, 1963.

8. Packard, Vance: Hidden Persuaders, New York, Pocket Books, 1958.

9. ———: Waste Makers, New York, Pocket Books, 1963.

10. Pearson, Gerald H.: Psychoanalysis and the Education of the Child, New York, Norton, 1954, pp. 232-233.

11. Symposium on Violence: Sponsored by the Med Correctional Ass, *in* Science Fortnightly, May 13, 1964.

Family Ties and the Money Tree

D. H. LAWRENCE'S SHORT STORY, "The Rocking Horse Winner," centers around Paul, a little English boy, who lives with his family in affluent circumstances, which they cannot afford. The father is a gentleman and the mother is a lady; both have very expensive tastes. Although both parents work, there is a chronic shortage of money and they cannot make enough to "keep up." The house becomes haunted by the unspoken phrase: "There must be more money! There must be more money!" Paul and his sisters live under the pall of this unspoken phrase. The mother contends that they do not have enough money because the family is unlucky. Little Paul tells his mother that he feels lucky, but his mother only laughs at him. While riding his big rocking horse, he keeps asking for the clue to "luck." He suddenly learns that if he races his rocking horse fast enough, the names of the winners of forthcoming horse races come mysteriously to him. He places bets through Bassett, the gardener, and wins again and again. Although he continues to win, it becomes ever more difficult for him to elicit the name of the winner. Finally he dies from exhaustion in a frantic but last successful attempt to force the name of the winner from his unknown source. Paul has been sending his winnings anonymously to his mother and only at his death does she learn the source of these funds. The little boy had given his life to get the house to stop whispering: "There must be more money!"

"The Rocking Horse Winner" is a painful commentary on family life in our society. No doubt, it takes a certain degree of affluence for people to complain about "there not being enough," especially when in the attempt to "keep up with the Joneses" no amount ever is enough. Possibly much of our buying, spending, and selling in this peculiarly affluent world is governed by a real or fancied sense of deprivation.

The notion of deprivation appears in all neurotic patients. In many, this feeling dates from early childhood. There is a story of a little boy who stood with his father by the cradle of his new baby brother. Gazing down at him and with pathos in his voice he said: "Dad, do you think there will be enough air for all of us to breathe?" If we exchange "air" for money, a similar concern echoes and reechoes through the behavior and attitudes of families.

When investigators for a national news magazine asked people what their biggest worry was, "money" and "making ends meet" were the predominant answers. Some clergymen report that in 75% of the cases in which people come to them with marital problems, money is an important factor. Likewise it does not take a physician long to learn that many of his patients' aches and pains are caused by financial stresses.

Money problems in most families have a solid basis in reality. The median income of families in the United States is $5,956, according to the latest figures of the US Department of Health, Education and Welfare. About 9.5 million families, or 20% of the 47 million families in the nation, had money incomes below $3,000 in 1962. The median income of nonwhite families was $3,330, as compared to $6,237 for white families. About

35 million of 200 million Americans today live in poverty.

The population of the United States increased by 40 million between 1950 and 1964. One half of this net growth in population occurred in the age group 5-19, which increased from 35 to 55 million. The population aged 65 and over also increased significantly from 12 to nearly 18 million. These substantial increases in the dependent population at both ends of the life span have laid heavy extra responsibilities on families.[3]

THE RELATION OF MONEY TO CHILD-REARING PRACTICES

Children are acutely aware of parental anxieties about money. They know when family income decreases or when one parent depreciates the other in terms of the management of money. Since the parents place so much importance on money, it creates in the child feelings of happiness and unhappiness, security and insecurity.[5]

In our culture, money is equated with security, love and achievement. Its absence is equated with deprivation. Feldman points out, however, that some differentials exist within our culture.[2] In the low-income group, the lack of money is brought rather directly to the child's knowledge. The child may have feelings of insecurity when his parents are worried about money, but he is usually clear about the fact that the insecurity is associated with money and not with his relationship to his parents. Feldman goes on to stress that the relatively free spending in this group when money is available, and the tendency to buy the child impractical or expensive things, create problems concerning spending money and often distort the child's values about necessities and luxuries.

In the middle-income groups, parents tend to conceal

money difficulties from their children. They use money to show love and approval, withhold it to mete out punishment. The child translates money and material things into symbols of love. Parental guilt about neglect or rejection of a child may be relieved by material over-indulgence. The parents view material acquisitions as signs of achievement, success, and status.

Often because of their own personality structures, parents are unable to meet the child's emotional needs or to handle child training problems constructively. Money may then become an instrument for manipulation and control, or a weapon for punishment. Forcing the child to atone for a misdeed or carelessness by de-priving him of money is inappropriate, since the pay-ment of money cannot in fact compensate for such ac-tions. Such tactics may lead the child to believe that any kind of conduct is acceptable as long as he can pay for it. Money may become a substitute for love. When money is used as a bargaining agent to secure the child's cooperation in doing his share of the family tasks, he is not being properly helped to achieve a sense of his importance, both as a receiving and as a con-tributing member of the family. When a child is bribed to put forth more effort in his school work, it empha-sizes the reward rather than personal development and the increased satisfaction that comes with achievement. In putting a monetary price on the child's good behav-ior or on his willingness to go to the doctor, parents set up false motivation.

Even more devastating is the use of bribes by parents in seeking to control the child's interpersonal relation-ships. I know a young teen-ager whose close friend was a boy of Mexican extraction. The family did not like "Mexicans" although they were willing to admit that this boy's behavior was exemplary in every way. They offered their son a variety of bribes, including a trip to Europe, to break up the friendship. The boy yielded to his parents. A series of circumstances later led the boy into psychotherapy. The acceptance of bribes, as in the incident described above as well as on other occasions, had given the boy a sense of self-betrayal, of injured integrity, and impaired self-confidence. He was aware that he had sold himself for a price and thereby given his parents a potent weapon of control over him. Similar cases abound in my files where parents attempt by bribes to control relationships of their children with the opposite sex, right up to and including marriage.

The child's attitude about the value of money can be easily obscured through the inappropriate use of money, namely its substitution for the basic elements in the parent-child relationship. Child specialists agree that a healthy growth experience for each child depends on the parents' differential use of money with siblings. Money for clothes and allowances should be related intelligently to the needs of children according to their respective ages. Money should not be used by parents to favor one sibling over another or to stimulate competitiveness. When money is used to stimulate performance, a variety of feelings is aroused in the child. The money he receives or fails to receive symbolizes parental acceptance or rejection, thus assuming unwarranted magnitude. To elicit the most money is to be the most favored child, but if he does attain this favored status, he suffers concomitant guilt.

When marital discord is present, the parents may compete with each other to buy the child's love. In the separation of parents or in a remarriage, the child may be caught in a multitude of money problems.

Many child specialists feel that our present prosperity accounts for the indiscriminate giving of too many material things to children. Neill, of the Summerhill School, cautions:

A child should not be given everything he asks for. Generally speaking, children today get far too much, so much that they cease having appreciation for a gift. Parents who overdo the giving of presents are often those who do not love their children enough. Such parents have to compensate by making a show of parental love, by showering expensive presents on their children much the same as a man who has been unfaithful to his wife will lavishly buy her a fur coat he can't afford.[6]

Many parents, because of their loneliness and dependency needs, seek to exert control over their grown children by sizeable gifts. Conflicts develop between the parents because one of them is giving secretly to a child. The adult child often strives to free himself from such control, but his success is too often accompanied by anxiety. To bolster his self-confidence, he goes on a spending spree, overextends his resources and develops an even deeper dependency on his parents.[2]

MONEY AND MARITAL DISCORD

Many a husband is "controlling" about money, holding his wife to a tight budget, doling out a meager allowance. In many cases this is a culturally determined role expectation. His father before him was the authoritative, thrifty provider. On the other hand, controlled disbursement of money may stem from the husband's recollections of hunger and deprivation in his youth.

In marital counseling, one often encounters a husband and wife who come from different backgrounds and have been emotionally conditioned to behave toward money in opposite ways. An example is the son of a widow from a small community where the motto was "wear it out or make it do." His mother, having to support herself and several children, drilled into her children the importance of putting some money aside for the inevitable rainy day. The boy married the daughter of an urban family in which the cultural values tended toward gracious living, "money is for spending" and "spend it now, it is later than you think" being the bywords. This couple, coming from such widely divergent backgrounds, did not understand each other's internalized attitudes toward money, and were on the verge of divorce. In such cases, the partners need the intellectual and emotional realization that the one is not trying deliberately to control or punish the other by exercising "silly notions" about money, but instead that he has been emotionally conditioned to behave this way. Then progress can be expected.

Some neurotic husbands may use money as a symbol of masculinity and power. In such cases the wife may retaliate against her husband's money behavior in various ways. She may make no effort to operate within the budget he has prescribed, or she may set limits of her own to meeting his sexual, physical or psychological needs. She may also spend money wastefully as a means of expressing hostility toward him.

A wife may use family or social standards to attack her husband's inadequacy in earning. If she has insatiable dependency needs, she may displace her feelings onto material things and make excessive demands on her husband. A demanding wife may force a husband into debt in an effort to placate her. Both husband and wife may use money to buy the other's love.

One of my patients used money as a weapon against her husband to relieve her profound feelings of resentment and rage. Periodically she wrote checks on her husband's bank account, almost exhausting the family's financial reserves, then denied having written them. The purchases she made were needless and extravagant. During treatment it became obvious that she was intensely angry with her husband. He was an engineer employed by a large company and was required to move frequently from one community to another. His wife was emotionally upset about this, as she wanted to live in the city where she was reared or, at least, in a neighboring community. She blamed her husband for her unhappiness and tried to persuade him to change jobs. His position with his company, however, was excellent and he could not afford to risk a change. His wife accepted none of his reasons, and harboring a chronic rage, began a career of subtle destructive acts not only toward her husband and family but toward herself as well, as money soon became the crux of family discord.

A wife working outside of the home may cause marital tension. Problems are usually minimal if the marital partners have common goals and work out a joint plan for the family income. Discord may develop, however, if a husband feels inadequate because his wife works. If he demands that she quit work, she may react strongly to the idea of giving up her employment with the status, independence, and satisfaction it affords her. A wife, on the other hand, may add to her husband's already existing feelings of inadequacy if she has to work to supplement his income.

Parental ties may be fashioned with money and woven into a knot too tight for either a young married couple or their parents easily to sever. When parents support an adult child who marries but continues his education, the ties are strengthened. When a young married couple continue to live in either of the parental homes, many types of dependency problems arise.

Rivalry between the two sets of parents is often expressed in outdoing each other in their gifts. When grandchildren arrive, relationships become even more complicated, money being used to buy love and control.

Equilibrium in marriage may be disturbed not only by a drop in income, but by an upward swing. Neither spouse may be able to tolerate the power that comes with increased income. At times, however, a marriage can be maintained only because the husband's good earning capacity enables him to meet his wife's narcissistic needs. Compulsive individuals often have difficulty in marriage because their basic rigidities in personality are reflected in their use of money.

The emotionally immature person who has no concept of money management is likely to encounter serious difficulty in marriage. He competes and fights with his wife on a sibling-rivalry basis. These competitive feelings render a person unable to share money realistically. The husband's immaturity may also interfere with his making a satisfactory vocational adjustment. His inadequacy prevents him from earning more money, and his failure fans the hostility and resentment of his dissatisfied wife. These factors operating together may inhibit any drive to seek more remunerative work, especially if the wife is ambitious and has high socioeconomic goals. One such husband yearned wistfully for the nurture of the situation implied in an American proverb: "Three faithful friends: an old wife, an old dog, and ready money."

THE USE OF MONEY BY THE SINGLE ADULT

Although the way single adults spend or save their money is essentially the same as the rest of the population having similar needs and standards, some variations in spending patterns exist for them and stem from the meaning money has for them. They frequently spend money for luxuries instead of necessities, since the luxuries serve as substitutes for love, companionship, family, and children. As Feldman well points out: "What appears on the surface to be self-indulgence may be a compensation for lacks in relationships and normal gratification of dependency needs. Loneliness may result in an undue preoccupation with extravagant living; the fancy apartment and lavish entertainment may be devices to relieve the anxiety loneliness engenders and to deny that one is really alone." [2] Single people often have difficulty in managing their money and in saving.

On the other hand, loneliness may mobilize a person's feelings of insecurity and make him fearful of spending money, since it is the only security he has. His efforts to save to provide for his old age may be so strenuous that he denies himself present satisfactions.

It is not suggested here that all persons living alone are lacking in healthy family attachments, spend money recklessly or are extremely penurious. A person living alone, however, does have additional spending needs. The lack of other persons with whom to share the costs of daily living means that his needs cannot be met as economically as those of a person living in the context of a family. Income tax rates are also higher for him.

OLDER PERSONS' USE OF MONEY

Older people, because of their forgetfulness and inability to recall recent events, may find it increasingly difficult to manage their economic resources successfully. They may become emotionally disturbed when they have to solve even minor problems relating to the uses of money. Some of these people long for a passive-dependent relationship with others taking over their care and relieving them of any concern about money matters. This is why some of the pension and monthly payment plans offered by church agencies are attractive to older persons, who surrender their property and receive money and/or care in return as long as they live. Others become anxious, fearful and depressed if they have to relinquish control of their funds. They have always enjoyed the power money gave them, and even if others help to manage their affairs, they want to feel that they can make the final decisions.

Some senile persons develop fear reactions when they imagine that their families, either to save the expense of caring for them or to gain control of their funds, are trying to do away with them. Such fears often nurture self-defensive behavior, difficult to manage in the family setting. One sees in older people many other forms of behavior. Some—perfectly well-off financially—feel so insecure that they hoard their resources to the point of miserliness. Others may literally throw their money away, sign blank checks, or give gifts to strangers. Some suddenly increase their scale of spending in order to enjoy in their declining years the luxuries and pleasures they previously denied themselves. They may draw up punitive wills, disinheriting their children or relatives for real or fantasied slights. As William Hazlitt remarked in his essay "On Making One's Will": "It is ordinarily the last opportunity a man has to express his contrariety."

Many an elderly person reacts peculiarly to a pension. The pension represents much less than he previously earned, and although his expenses are also much less he gets the feeling that he is poor. Since money usually stands for independence, he may be unwilling to spend what he has.

The widow with an adequate pension may have difficulty managing it because of the contradictory meanings it has for her. After a lifetime of frugality and self-denial, she cannot change her way of living in spite of the arguments her children may advance to convince her that she can spend every cent she receives. Her counter arguments are: "What will be left for you if I do that?" or "Your father never liked that kind of waste." Thus she continues to live on an inadequate income. "Leaving something" stands for a kind of immortality. As long as she spends little on herself she can give a good account of her behavior.

PLANNING AND TRAINING IN MONEY MANAGEMENT

Increased understanding of psychological and cultural motivations in regard to behavior has made it obvious that money is a significant factor in the social adjustment of families, irrespective of their economic status. Research has substantiated the observation that the development of sound family attitudes toward money does not depend so much on the amount of income as on how each partner uses the income. Modern families reflect the values of our democratic society.[1] Usually the interests and well-being of all family members are considered, and each is included in planning the use of the income. The marriage relationship is more flexible in money matters and less institutionalized than in the past, and therefore can be a mutual search for fulfillment of such deep human needs as love and security.

The family's mode of living is determined by the goals the husband and wife set for themselves. These goals, of course, influence the expenditure of the family's money, time, and energy. Thoughtful planning, based on actual and potential income, is essential if the family is to meet smoothly its present and future responsibilities. Intelligent planning by the husband and wife, with some consultation with the children, will enable them to make constructive use of the economic devices that our society has developed. They will also be able to use money creatively and thereby escape the pressures and anxieties that come with the misuse of money. All families should have on their walls a statement by Dominique Bouhours: "Money is a good servant but a dangerous master."

An encouraging development for the family has been the introduction in some of our schools of courses in consumer education. The need for this is cogently illustrated in this excerpt from a letter written to a high school principal by a former student:

I want to know why you and your teachers did not tell and teach about life and the hard, critically practical world. . . . I wish I had been taught more about family relationships, paying off a small mortgage, household mechanics, the chemistry of food, how to budget and live within a budget, the value of insurance, how to figure interest when borrowing money and paying it back in small installments, how to detect shoddy goods, how to be thrifty, how to resist high pressure salesmanship, how to buy economically and intelligently.[4]

Spurred by the urgent, widespread need for consumer education, Lincoln High School in Yonkers has begun to expose students to a dramatic experimental course in consumer economics.[7, 8] Students taking the course explore such bread-and-butter subjects as the comparative costs of building, buying or renting a house; the dollar-and-cents difference between saving to buy or using the installment plan; interest costs of buying a used car on time; how to fill out income tax forms; how to spot gyps and frauds and so on. In classrooms, the students study actual installment sales contracts and insurance policies, and fill out actual tax forms.

Field work is included in the experimental course. Students shop in local stores or businesses to learn how to compare prices and values. For example, two students went to a used car lot to check prices and installment contracts. They expressed interest in a car, and asked what it would cost on a two-year installment plan. After the salesman gave them the figure, they computed the true annual interest charge and found it was 47%. When they questioned the salesman about this high rate, he became angry and chased them off the lot.

The school invites businessmen, bankers, government officials, insurance agents and other experts to address school assemblies on a variety of consumer topics. Probably, the most creative part of the school's effort in consumer education is its success in incorporating financial training directly into the regular curriculum. An English teacher, for example, will examine the persuasion techniques used by advertisers. A mathematics teacher will lecture on consumer credit contracts, interest rates, mortgages, taxes, scholarships, loans, and will devise many problems around these topics for the students to solve. A science teacher will probe health advertising and the chemistry of products ranging from water softeners to insecticides. Social studies, industrial art and other departments of the school have no difficulty introducing effectively into their courses many aspects of consumer education.

Unfortunately because of the apathy of tradition-bound school administrators, most schools will be slow in adopting such programs. Notwithstanding, the success of Lincoln's experiment warrants the attention of the nation's educators.

CONCLUSION

Cultural anthropologists have shown by the study of a variety of societies that certain values are transmitted almost exclusively through the family. By precept and example, any idea planted in the child's mind can be nurtured and reenforced. Within the family, therefore, the practical aspects of money management can most easily be learned.

It is an urgent task to guide the affluence and materialism of our society into constructive and creative channels. Although in our Age of Leisure the pursuit of happiness is the validated ticket handed to the young, the child must not get the impression that he has the right to live his life without regard for others. Unfortunately, a child is often deceived into believing that when he has enough money he can buy happiness, or that to possess things makes one happy. By this token, he may look forward to automatic contentment through automated machinery. In the family, the child can also learn that the proper use of money sustains the tradition of love, grace and service. In the socializing process, the child can acquire growing contentment in sharing the advantages with which he has been blessed.

Modern psychiatry stresses the importance of sharing, for clinical studies indicate that man cannot keep his balance, mature his faculties or fulfill his needs as a human being unless he learns to share. This means sharing one's possessions, one's love, and one's self. Altruistic parents lead to altruistic children. If the value systems of parents are grounded in the Judeo-

Christian tradition, their acceptance and cherishing of their children will make of the home an ideal setting for the development of responsible citizenship.

REFERENCES CHAPTER 4

1. Desmonde, William H.: Magic, Myth and Money. The Origin of Money in Religious Ritual, New York, Free Press, 1962.

2. Feldman, Frances Lomas: The Family in a Money World, New York, Family Service Ass of America, 1957.

3. Giving, USA. A Compilation of Facts Related to American Philanthropy, New York, Amer Ass of Fund Raising Counsel, 1965, pp. 43-44.

4. Hunt, Herold C.: Bull Nat Ass Secondary-School Principals, October, 1960, p. 153.

5. Lauterbach, Albert: Man, Motives, and Money. Psychological Frontiers of Economics, ed. 2, Ithaca (NY), Cornell Univ Press, 1959.

6. Neill, A. S.: Summerhill: A Radical Approach to Child Rearing, New York, Hart, 1960.

7. Porter, Sylvia: Consumer Education, New York Post, August 11, 1965, p. 32.

8. Schoenfeld, David, and Mendenhall, James E., eds.: Consumer Education in Lincoln High School, Mount Vernon (NY), Consumers Union of US, 1965.

The Anatomy of Giving

W HEN CHARLES MERRILL, a directing partner of the stock brokers, Merrill Lynch, Pierce, Fenner and Smith, died on October 6, 1956, he left an estate estimated at twenty-five million dollars. He had already taken care of his family, and during the last quarter century of his life had given away millions of dollars to charities and institutions. By his wish, the final estate, which he called "his bundle," was to be divided "five per cent to personal friends and ninety-five per cent to colleges, churches, hospitals and causes I love."

Charles Merrill was a keen executive and astute investor; he was also both philosophical and human in the finest sense of these words. Not long before he died he stated:

It is a funny thing about the United States and the people who live in it. They work hard, they fight hard, they scratch, they bite, they yell and they scream—and then when they kick the bucket they give it all away. That is something that other nations simply cannot get through their heads. What makes us tick? I think the thing that makes us tick is that we love our country, we love our fellow man and we love to serve our neighbors and make them happy, just as we serve the members of our family.[2]

In this richest of countries a great deal of money is given away—hundreds of millions of dollars annually. That being so, a natural question is: "What governs or inhibits the urge to give, and what are the appeals that really move people?" Obviously the motivation behind giving involves a wide and complex range of emotion and intent: self-interest, family honor, sympathy, pity, guilt, fear, snob appeal, altruism, patriotism, immortality. Appeals designed to induce people to give are geared to reach many individuals and groups, and are based on the recognition that most gifts come from combined rather than simple motives. Attempts to deal with giving in objective terms have been increasingly complicated by the discovered and now axiomatic truth: "People give to people—not to causes." Thus when a cause is presented, the prospective giver must be able to see which people are involved in and behind the cause.

PSYCHODYNAMICS OF GIVING

The Human Spirit and Giving. The American Association of Fund-Raising Counsel, in categorizing motivational theories and insights in giving, designated one category as "human spirit." [19] The bases for giving in this category are: love of God, love of one's fellow man, and social responsibility. These givers include sincerely religious people, those who having attained economic security have a sense of social duty, those who are nearing the end of their lives, those who want a better tomorrow, creative givers, and altruists in general.

Motivated by spiritual conviction, dynamic idealism, responsible citizenship, institutional loyalty, and compassion for the less fortunate, these persons seek certain specific goals through giving. Among these are the preservation of past accomplishments, the elevation of standards, and the perpetuation of a loved or respected name. The impulse to leave a permanent memorial to a loved one (often one's self) is well known to institutions seeking large capital gifts and bequests in the wills of wealthy friends and benefactors.

It is recognized that the "human spirit" type of giver will give in response to a carefully documented statement of the case, or to a personal appeal by a well-informed advocate of the cause seeking aid, or by a social equal. Such givers are amenable to suggested giving standards and respond to dramatized presentations, continued information and cultivation, and identification symbols. The "human spirit" motive can be encompassed fairly well by the term *humanitarianism*: human sympathy and a rational element of social responsibility. Brotherly love, community spirit, interest in good causes are all different aspects of unselfish altruism. Karl Menninger stresses that "Money-giving is a very good criterion . . . of a person's mental health. Generous people are rarely mentally ill people." [6]

Charles A. Anger, of the John Price Jones Company, has suggested one of the reasons an individual identifies with the good:

For many people, philanthropy offers the best opportunity they have to identify themselves with the finer part of their nature. This gives them an opportunity to share in the cultural and socially valuable things in our civilization which they themselves have not had a chance to participate in because of business pressures. You might call this a kind of synthetic upgrading of the individual's personality, compensating for early hopes and ambitions sacrificed in order to make a living.[1]

Thus, whether one gives out of gratitude, or because he wants to help his neighbor, for atonement, or for personal salvation, or even from a sense of guilt—he is involving himself in community responsibility and public service.

The Self-Interest Emotions Motivating Giving. Dr. Abel Hanson, who was in charge of Alumni giving at

Teachers College, Columbia University, has stressed self-interest as a common motive in giving.[14] Thus, if an individual is allowed freedom in giving, his gifts will reflect his particular concerns, and vary in proportion to the impact of the appeal on his self-interest. Emotions concerned with fear or self-preservation often induce people to give their money. Such slogans as, "Two out of five will die," "Give for your health's sake," "Don't let this happen to your child" often motivate people to give. Then, too, many people are afraid not to give because of social and business criticism.

Guilt may also be a motivating factor in giving. In German, *Schuld* may mean either *debt* or *guilt*. Successful self-assertion through money-making is often followed by generous gifts to charities and foundations, not only to save taxes but for the good of one's soul. Alfred Nobel's early experiments with explosives resulted in a nitroglycerin blast that killed his younger brother and was responsible for his father's stroke. For the balance of his life Nobel was a lonely and melancholic person, without friends. Both before and after establishing the Nobel Prizes, he sought escape in writing fiction. Thus the motivation for philanthropic giving by successful businessmen may range from feelings of responsibility to those of guilt or frustration.

A man in a high income bracket may contribute substantially to evade taxes. His motivation is clear; his only problem is a matter of judicious choosing between causes. Then there is the individual who gives, glowing with the promise of publicity, honor rolls, acknowledgments, memorials or recognition by a social or business superior.

Among the types who can be induced to give out of self-interest are the fearful, the socially ambitious, the *nouveau riche*, and the go-getter in business. Ethically debatable as their vanity, ambition and motives of self-advancement may be, their benefactions are nonetheless of high social use.

Religious Motivation for Giving. Organized religion feels that the ultimate worth of any gift is to be found in the motive behind the gift, "for as a man thinketh in his heart, so is he" (Proverbs 23:7). There has developed in the church a philosophy of Christian stewardship based on the biblical meanings of the word *steward.* The name first is given to the overseer, foreman, or manager of a property that he does not own but over which he is "steward" for his Lord (Genesis 43:19, 44:1-4; I Chronicles 28:1; Matthew 20:8, Luke 12:42, 16:1-8). The second is found in such passages as I Corinthians 4:1, Titus 1:7, and I Peter 4:10, where the individual is admonished to be a faithful steward of "the mysteries of God" and of "the manifold Grace of God." The church's program interlinks both forms of stewardship.

Some basic principles regarding stewardship can be drawn from the Old Testament. Chief among these is that God is the owner of all property and that man is subject to Him in all things. Thus man is only a steward of God's property.* Man's ownership is a limited one,

---

* The biblical concept of property extends to life itself and to viewing it as a cherished gift. While I was visiting Bergen, Norway, a guide told me of a family living on a small farm, located outside of Bergen on the top of a mountain. The altitude and terrain were such that horses could not be used. A two-hour walk was required to reach the top of the mountain from the point where transportation stopped. No modern conveniences were available. The family was independent in that they made essentially everything they needed or used. The mother even knitted as she climbed up or down the mountain. An American tourist, after hearing and seeing something of the family's hardships and struggles, asked the mother: "Does it pay to live here and put up with all of this?" She replied without a moment's hesitation: "Life itself is pay enough."

never to be regarded as an end in itself or as an absolute right. Property is used for the proper exercise of one's responsibilities in society and for the benefit and welfare of all. Today this doctrine is probably most prevalent among those who till the soil. People who abuse the soil are criticized by their neighbors. 4-H Clubs and Future Farmers of America (FFA) imbue their members with the philosophy that the soil must not be sapped of its fertility nor allowed to be eaten away by erosion, but must be cared for and passed on as a precious heritage to the next generation.

Further, the biblical prophetic challenge is that property be held and used in keeping with the radical demands of God for justice, mercy and faithfulness. Tithes, offerings and other forms of systematic giving should be carried out in grateful response to the goodness, mercy and grace of God.

The admonition to tithe and offer first fruits existed through various periods of Israel's history. Usually tithing was associated with some form of taxation, because of the close connection between religion and the state in ancient Israel. Some Old Testament illustrations are Abraham giving a tithe to Melchizedek (Genesis 14:20); the tithe appointed by Hezekiah chiefly for the support of the clergy (II Chronicles 31:2-21); the supervised collection of tithes stored and utilized for the support of the clergy and the maintenance of the cultus (Nehemiah 12:44-47, 13:4-14). Tithing practices, of course, varied through Israel's history, taking a multiplicty of forms and meanings.

Those who have studied giving in the Christian Church contend that the early Christians were motivated by compassion to relieve the suffering of the poor and the sick, and to share the gospel with the world. Today a variety of motives, both secular and religious, could be listed for giving to the church and to other religious causes. Among them, oblation holds a prominent place; people have often had the impulse to give to the church in order to assure their own salvation. This motive has been prevalent in the church throughout the ages.

The fear motive is closely related to the oblation motive. Fear of hell and purgatory induces many people to give. Many also give out of fear of what God's punishment might do to them if they are unfaithful. This strain from an early English rhyme emphasizes the need to placate the Lord:

> For lambe, pig and calf, and for other the like,
> Tithe so as thy cattle the Lord do not strike.

The present-day church would reject fear in a Christian philosophy of stewardship, putting the emphasis instead on "love that casteth out all fear."

Personal glorification is a factor in religious as well as in other forms of giving. In the pew-rent system of the early American church, a man's social position was indicated by the pew he occupied. Today, when individual gifts are made public and subscription lists are published, people gain recognition and enhanced personal prestige. The desire for these may be the main motivating factors in some giving, despite the admonishment in the Bible that one give in such a way that one's left hand know not what one's right hand is doing and that one not parade one's goodness or seek recognition for good deeds (Matthew 6:1-4).

Self-interest, however, is frankly emphasized in the promotional propaganda for benevolent work. An example is the Marshall Plan, which was justified by the promise that feeding the world would counteract the spread of communism. Efforts to raise money for missionaries have also stressed that missionaries are fighters of communism. The drive for self-preservation is a strong one, and although it may not be the noblest motive, the church could not expect to be free of its presence.

While the missionary motive has been to spread the gospel, at times a country has enjoyed some material and temporal returns for its missionary effort, such as the development of new trade areas. Many servicemen in World War II realized the value of missions when they were assisted by Christian natives. Van Dusen discussed this in his book, *They Found the Church There*.[20] At times, some church leaders have equated the "returns" from missions with the reasons for missions.

Personal profit is also an old motive for religious giving. Many believe that if they conduct their business on a Christian basis, they are likely to prosper. A number of prominent men have testified publicly how they have prospered when they began to run their business as if Christ were a partner. Luther P. Powell, in *Money and the Church*, writes: "However, when a man is motivated to take Christ as a member of the firm in order to become more prosperous, Christ is not being glorified, he is being exploited." [15] Powell goes on to discuss the testimonies of a number of men in the past fifty years who have claimed tithing to have brought them material blessings.

The Church is rightfully disturbed by any tendency on the part of people to bargain with God, and firmly emphasizes that bargaining has no place in the worship and devotion of the religious person. The biblical record does report that the Israelites were urged to give because God had redeemed them from Egypt and had given them a land that flowed with milk and honey.

This "giving," however, must be interpreted as a sacrifice of love and gratitude, not one of bargaining.

One of the most colorful chapters in religious giving has been written by the Mormon Church. "The earth is the Lord's and the fullness thereof" is the cornerstone of its program. In acknowledgment of the supreme possessorship so declared, the great Landlord requires of His tenants a rental of their time and substance. In acknowledgment of their relation as tenants to Him as Owner, church members are commanded to devote specifically one-seventh of their time, one day in seven, to His exclusive service. Of their substance and the increase thereof, the Lord calls for a tenth, the tithe. Thus the Latter-day Saints profess to be observers of the law of the tithe. This requirement is not directly based on the tithe-paying included in the Mosaic code, but on that law as reestablished in the Mormon Church. In the *Book of Mormon* is found this admonition and promise:

But before ye seek for riches, seek ye for the kingdom of God. And after ye have obtained a hope in Christ ye shall obtain riches, if ye seek them; and ye will seek them for the intent to do good—to clothe the naked, and to feed the hungry, and to liberate the captive, and administer relief to the sick and the afflicted (Jacob 2:18-19).

Motivated by the tenets of their faith, the Mormons have developed a Church Welfare Plan so extensive and effective that they are able to assist any of their people in need wherever they may be.[5] The plan is completely divorced from any governmental or political affiliation; it is wholly a Church Plan, based on religious principles and carried out entirely by Church instrumentalities and agencies. Basic to the plan are religious convictions built on God's universal command given to all men through ancient Israel in the Wilderness: "Thou shalt love thy neighbor as thyself" (Lev. 19:18).

Giving and Power. Dr. Ernest Dichter, founder and president of the Institute for Motivational Research, observed during his studies that when somebody is asked to give money, the emotion mobilized is: "I am capable of giving money." Dichter goes further: "*When we give, we play God.* We feel very 'uppity.' We're very arrogant." [8]

Thus, giving or not giving becomes an assertion of one's power and is related to attitudes that emanate from early parent-child relationships. A child can give or not give and affect parents thereby. In giving or not giving at his will, as in toilet training, the child maintains power over the parent. When an adult is asked to give, then, he is asked to repeat a situation in which he was involved when a child: "If I give in to Mommy, then I give up my power and the secret of my power." It is not difficult to understand how toilet training may have become a serious power struggle in any person's early life. As long as a child did not give in to the attempts at training on the part of mother or father, he withheld the secret.

Gradually, the child learned that cooperation brings reward, also. With successful toilet training came self-esteem, a new feeling of accomplishment, and a new and rewarding relationship with mother and father. Thus, by surrendering a little of his power, he had actually received a greater power. As a result of the power struggle that might have taken place in early childhood, an individual may fear that giving in some way causes him to lose power. Thus, the emphasis that should be made openly and frankly, according to Dichter, is that *giving buys power.* The individual realizes this when it is called to his attention. His giving makes him a participant in the organization he is supporting, and thus gains him the privilege of sharing in the policies of the organization and of criticizing its actions.

Dichter feels that psychologically one always gives either to mother or to father, or possibly to an uncle, and from a psychological standpoint, one never gives as readily to an anonymous person or cause. Perhaps this is why colleges have been successful in obtaining funds from their alumni; after all, they are giving to their *alma mater*.

A flagrant use of parental symbols in fund-raising campaigns can be observed in the Mothers March on Polio. By sending *mothers* out to seek gifts from neighbors, the organization offers *1.* a psychological mother with whom the giver can identify as both a parent and a child; *2.* a symbol of protection for one's self as well as for one's children; and *3.* a neighbor who threatens status loss for refusal, and offers recognition for cooperation. Often attractive girls are instructed to show special attention to men who are asked to give to a cause. The obvious reward for giving is an enhanced sense of virility.

To some extent, present-day psychological studies affirm Dichter's concept of the relationship of giving to power. Contrary to Dichter, however, others minimize the selfish, egoistic component of childhood narcissism, and perceive the phenomenon of giving as one of the highest forms of selfless love.

LAWS OF GIVING

In the *YMCA Magazine* of February, 1952, Harold J. Seymour set forth four laws governing giving: [18]

1. *Giving begets giving.* Thus, the best prospects for gifts are an organization's present givers.

2. *Giving is prompted emotionally before it is rationalized.* Sheer data should never be permitted to crowd out the emotional component. Even the arguments for the collection of taxes are of secondary value to the emotional appeals. Since people tend to respond to successful patterns, fund-raising is best conducted in an atmosphere of universality, optimism and dramatization. In general, people like to join in a common cause whether they are rich or poor. Since giving is prompted emotionally before it is rationalized, certain guidelines emerge for approaching a prospective donor: solicitation should be personal; advocacy depends on loyalty and responsibility, which, in turn, depend on participation in the program; and voluntary efforts have a limited attention period.

3. *Giving is responsive.* The amount of giving is almost directly proportionate to the degree to which the approach is personal. Success, therefore, hinges on the quality of the leadership and the degree to which the solicitors are representative of the community. People are most likely to contribute when asked by a peer with whom they are in frequent personal contact. This explains why national appeals do better when the solicitation grows out of each local community. The most successful solicitors of funds for a particular cause are those who have themselves been thoroughly indoctrinated in that cause. There is no escape from the process of sustaining attention and interest, arousing confidence and conviction, inculcating the active desire to make a gift. Campaigners must be constantly aware of the laws of human inertia. Even when the desire to give is genuine and compelling, the candidate must be made to feel the urgency to give *now*. Men respond when an emergency is described, a deadline emphasized, a specific goal named. Givers are also encouraged by knowing what others are giving.

4. *Giving is variable.* Giving tends to fall into self-imposed habit patterns. Some give from a deep sense of

social responsibility. Others give generously, but sporadically and thoughtlessly. Then there are the conformers who give merely from a sense of duty. Unfortunately, some men are wholly selfish and negative about giving to any cause.

In general, givers want to know that their gifts will result in the greatest good to the greatest number. Their material gifts are made with the intention of uplifting man's spirit. Givers often need to be reassured that their gifts have not been measured so much by institutional safety as they have by services that benefit the entire community. As a result, many donors testify that their gifts have been like "bread cast on the waters."

Donors can be grouped into four types: *a.* thoughtful givers, *b.* generous givers, *c.* conforming givers, and *d.* selfish givers. This is a practical type of grouping used by fund-raising specialists such as Seymour.[17-18] To this group should be added a catch-all: the giver with mixed motives, whose giving may not be singular in purpose.

Among thoughtful givers are those whose giving is motivated by a sense of social responsibility. They contribute out of a desire to sustain fundamental values, to effect desirable changes, to do justice, or to further an ideal. Such individuals usually have a deep social consciousness and a broad social outlook. Often well past the stage when one is interested merely in making money, these persons are activated by "philanthropy" in its literal sense. They want facts, weigh them carefully, rarely act swiftly. They require a thorough presentation of the case by one or more persons who have expert knowledge and good taste.

Generous givers are actually not more generous than thoughtful givers, but are motivated by sheer loyalty, sympathy, gratitude or conscience. They are usually warm-hearted, naturally generous, often impulsive. They respond to dramatization of a need and follow the examples of others. They require systematic cultivation, followed by personal solicitation from a business or social equal.

Conforming givers are rarely included in the special-gifts phase of a capital campaign because giving large sums is seldom activated by motivations of pure habit and conformity. These givers respond to obligations of membership, and are supporters of established patterns. They give according to past performance and in proportion to a real or supposed average. They are the unimaginative followers who respond only to the appeal for universality, but like their names to appear on the list of donors to maintain their place among those whose esteem they desire to win or hold.

Selfish givers are motivated by such mixed emotions as fear and vanity. A sharp distinction cannot, of course, always be made between self-interest and selfishness. Enlightened self-interest is psychologically healthy. Selfishness, on the other hand, implies an extreme self-centeredness and is considered emotionally unhealthy. Selfish givers are socially deaf. They are usually moved more by fear of public opinion than by any good their giving will do. The approach to a person in this category, for a special gift, should be by two or more business or social superiors. Selfish givers occasionally make spectacular gifts; consequently this group should not be overlooked.

Givers with mixed motivation include a sizeable group among contributors to any worthy cause. Feelings of ambivalence toward almost any cause are commonplace. Some individuals are consistently helpful to other people, but with ulterior motives. They may be doing penance, covering up for present wickedness, making friends in order to take advantage of them later, or seeking prestige. Although the motives of such individuals are questionable, they must be given credit where their actions are of positive value to society. As Berne aptly points out, people can cover up for past wickedness by becoming more wicked, take advantage of people by fear rather than generosity, and seek prestige through ways evil rather than good.[3] The ubiquitous braggarts give for competitive rather than benevolent reasons; they boast loudly of having given more property or money than anyone else. Their motives need not be questioned; after all, they are competing in a constructive way. In the Book of Ecclesiastes is written, "There is not a righteous man on earth who does good and never sins" (Eccl. 7:20). Theologians have interpreted this to mean, "There is no man wholly free of sin when he is doing good."[4] In other words, self-interest is involved to some degree, no matter how small, in every human good deed. Reinhold Niebuhr points out the same ambivalence in individuals: "The final enigma of history is not how the righteous will gain victory over the unrighteous, but how the evil in every good and the unrighteousness of the righteous is to be overcome."[13]

GUIDING PRINCIPLES TO STIMULATE GIVING

The John Price Jones Company has identified some guiding principles in fund-raising, which reveal much about motivation in giving.[7,10]

The immediate job is to *cultivate* the prospective donor, *not to solicit gifts*. One must stimulate curiosity, interest, and then a desire to participate. The best person for creating an interest in the project may not necessarily be the best one to solicit the gift. Stating the case formally and publicly may not be sufficient to bring the best results. The prospective donor must be cultivated by another human being as intimately as possible, and motivated by him.

Steps must be planned in advance to bring a prospective benefactor closer to a project by increasing his knowledge and by inviting his participation in the affairs of the organization seeking support. The old English proverb is especially apropos in such a situation: "He that gives his heart will not deny his money."

Soliciting too soon may bring poor results. At times it takes months, even years, to arouse sufficient interest to justify a major gift. Specialists in fund-raising report that many failures are caused by a committeeman overestimating the degree of interest shown by a prospective benefactor and soliciting too soon. The late Daniel Willard is reported to have said to an impatient fund-raiser who wanted to move faster on institutional finance: "You can get two or three crops a year if you want to raise alfalfa. But you have to allow a lot more time than that if you're raising an oak."

Preliminary cultivation is carried out best in a relaxed, informal setting. A few well-planned comments at a social gathering, on the golf course, over a cup of coffee or at the country club may stimulate the interest of the prospect more quickly than a formal meeting, a letter or printed literature. The special interests of one's prospects should be accurately determined. In this way wealthy persons can be guided to recognize an existing need and may make a substantial contribution to the cause. Experience has proved that interest in making a gift is initially aroused by the *broad educational or social welfare mission* and not by the specific building or facility needed. Furthermore, when a prospective donor's interest is aroused, it is easier to discuss the specific need, not the cost of the project.

The best method of securing major gifts for an institution such as a university is to have potential givers personally and formally identified with the university. One takes greatest interest in the things in which one has a personal, participating responsibility. Thus the crucial approach is to find a sincerely useful place within the university family for each of the prospects. The aim should be to build the prospects into the university program rather than simply to tack them on. Most potential benefactors, because of their economic, cultural or professional positions, have more to offer a university than money. The prospects should not be given the impression that they are wanted within the university structure solely because of their favored financial position.

A person usually does not give substantially unless and until he is deeply motivated. He must have the desire to give. The institution or the project has to mean something to him personally and emotionally, as well as intellectually.

Recording, acknowledging and expressing appreciation for gifts is the lifeblood of future support. These should be done promptly and properly, for they are the best incentives for the donor's next gift. Besides the official notices, donors should be personally thanked by all the individuals who had anything to do with obtaining their gifts.

A factor in giving or soliciting funds, which may transcend all those listed by fund raisers, is how deeply the solicitor believes in the cause he represents. A civic leader once said that the three most difficult things for a person to do are to climb a fence leaning toward him, kiss a girl leaning away from him, and sell something he does not believe in. Accomplishment in fund-raising, when one believes in the cause one represents, is no more poignantly illustrated than in the life of Martha Berry and the school she established for the mountain people of the South. Harnett T. Kane tells her story with great insight in *Miracle in the Mountains*. In spite of continuous obstacles, her commitment to the cause she represented impelled her to search repeatedly for every source of funds, to tell her story to all who would listen, and to invite prospective donors to join in her great enterprise. The present splendid school, with its remarkable heritage, is enduring evidence of her *charisma:* an ability to recreate her own vision in the minds of others.

PHILANTHROPY

The word philanthropy comes from the Greek, *philos anthropos*, meaning love of mankind, practical benevolence toward men in general, the disposition or active effort to promote the happiness and well-being of one's fellowmen.*

A few centuries ago a large number of Europe's displaced persons fled to a new country and began new lives. This venture came to be known as the Great American Experiment. The group's Declaration of Independence in 1776 set forth its philosophy, and its Constitution of 1789 declared its principles of freedom and the methods whereby it intended to live in peace with all men. To a great extent, this democracy was founded by our forefathers as a civic expression of their

* Thoreau, in *Walden*, describes how charitable enterprises often violate the classical meaning of philanthropy. He enunciated this principle: "If you give money, spend yourself with it. . . ."

religious faith. Benevolence and kindness became an integral part of American life. To see a need was to meet it with direct individual attention, and usually without delay.

Numerous Americans take seriously their obligation of brotherhood by seeking to alleviate suffering and to raise the standard of living. Private philanthropy has flourished where initiative and individual freedom are most respected. With its freedoms and free enterprise system, America has furnished fertile soil for the phenomenal evolution of philanthropists, who take pleasure in giving away billions of dollars every year. The 1967 edition of *Giving USA* estimates that American philanthropy in 1966 totaled thirteen billion six hundred million dollars.[11] Of the $13.6 billion given during 1966, gifts from individuals accounted for $10,600,000,000; from foundations, $1,250,000,000; from business firms, $800,000,000; and from charitable bequests $926,000,000. The $13.6 billion was distributed as follows: 48% to religious purposes; 18% to health and hospitals; 17% to education; 5% to private welfare programs; 4% to civic and cultural; and 8% to "other purposes."

The American spirit of "help thy neighbor" is a tradition with roots that go back to the frontier days of roof-raisings, community defense, quilting parties, and husking bees. It is estimated that fifty million men, women and young people are giving their services for a wide variety of worthy causes. These include the housewife who rings doorbells on behalf of community projects, the corporation executive or professional man who serves a hospital, university or church as committee member or trustee, the recreation leader who gives nights and weekends to a teenage canteen, and endless others. The unique American drive to get things done without government assistance, coupled with a fabulous organizing genius, accounts for this phenomenal success. With such examples, civic traits are acquired by each oncoming generation. Volunteer fund-raising is an excellent preparation for active citizenship.

Probably business executives account for the greatest number of volunteers. Recent surveys of the National Industrial Conference Board show that executives of American business corporations devote at least 40% of their time dealing with problems not directly related to their jobs, but which, however, affect company policy and philosophy with respect to government and civic affairs, community relations, company contributions, and education.

From biblical days through the last century, philanthropy was a matter of alms-giving for the poor and needy. Today, and for the past several years, while government has taken over the task of improving man's lot, philanthropy has projected itself into new activities such as extending educational opportunities and developing cultural programs. Even in medicine where giving has been more exclusively for prevention and cure of disease, some attention is now being devoted to a study of well human beings as a guide in dealing with social problems such as delinquency and crime.

If philanthropy were suspended, our American Way of Life would be jeopardized, for philanthropy is woven into our life patterns, through its contributions to education, religion, and social activities. All of us are indebted to it. Who among us has paid the full cost of his education and free libraries, his churches, hospitals and other cultural essentials? The list of good things available to us at essentially no personal cost is infinite. Although most of our philanthropic benefactors are unknown to us, we are the recipients of their benevolence, just as our progeny will be the recipients of ours.

It is part of the American Way of Life that givers are

allowed freedom of choice in their giving. Our government permits a wealthy man to choose between giving to the government through taxes on his estate or giving to further the welfare of mankind by tax-exempt philanthropic gifts. He is free to make his choice, and the court will respect his decision. The growth of philanthropy attests to the increasing maturity and intelligent idealism of our people. Among philanthropists, "the art of wise giving" is more than a catch-phrase. One generous giver, Mr. Julius Rosenwald, has said: "Viewing the matter in retrospect, I can testify that it is nearly always easier to make one million dollars honestly than to dispose of it wisely."

Motivations underlying philanthropic giving cover a wide range. Lauterbach, for example, has written of the defensive needs of business in the United States. He sees businessmen as a group constantly seeking self-justification through involvement in enterprises of social utility.[12] These defensive needs have a direct bearing on the success of the programs of giving carried out in almost all industries and businesses.

In many other parts of the world, however, such as most of the Arab and Latin American countries, there are few signs of defensive business attitudes. Large profits are made and tremendous wealth accumulated by a small minority. This minority feels no need to justify this accumulated wealth to the millions of people who live in squalor. Lauterbach contends that business in most parts of Europe remains quiet about its activities and profits.[12]

The motivation of business activity has been changing since the beginning of capitalism in the United States. In the early days of our history, making money was considered a kind of transcendental calling. This was partly a result of Calvinist influence. A period of rugged individualism followed when rough-and-tumble buccaneering was regarded as something of a social as well as an individual virtue. Then business developed into Big Business, which found it expedient to develop either a genuine sense of responsibility or the appearance of such. The Better Business Bureaus represent an organized attempt to regulate the conduct of business to ethical and social norms. The important outlet for social responsibility became philanthropic giving. Suspicion regarding public welfare policies persisted despite their tremendous effectiveness. But the great structure of private philanthropy has been wholeheartedly welcome from the beginning. In her Christmas, 1949, column in the *New York Times*, Anne O'Hare McCormick wrote:

It's a funny thing about Santa Claus. At Christmas time everybody loves the jolly and benevolent old gentleman who delights the hearts of children. . . . But when a government is called a Santa Claus it is a term of opprobrium. . . . Generosity, in short, is regarded as a noble attribute in individuals but as a vice and weakness in nations.

Major changes have taken place in corporate giving in recent years. The present tax structure has strongly influenced the trend in corporation gifts. Philanthropy can be an inexpensive way to buy good will. Also, today there is less resistance than in the past to "giving away the stockholders' money," especially in those areas that feel subjected to explicit or implicit pressures from consumers. Much corporate giving appears to favor community agencies or research institutes that are of definite interest to the company, but a gradual broadening of the horizon of giving is taking place. This new pattern of giving often takes place through company foundations and is more businesslike than were some earlier patterns of philanthropy. The motivation for giving on the part of business points to an increased awareness either of social responsibilities or of moral defense needs.

Because of this highly business-like approach to giving practiced by company as well as private foundations, those who solicit funds from these sources must develop formidable skills.* The ablest solicitors of large gifts have had much in common in their philosophies and techniques. Each has known the cause he represented thoroughly and has believed in it with infectious sincerity. Each has talked in terms of ideas rather than money, has aimed high, and has had optimistic faith and supreme patience. Each has also been modest in his statements and considerate of the feelings and point of view of the prospective donor.

CONCLUSION

Giving involves a broad range of human motivations, gifts almost always coming from a combination of basic motivations. "People's memories. . . . people's fears. . . . people's sense of the appropriate" [9] play a part. Motivation may come from man's need for secur-

---

* Generally a man must be high in the business world before he is in a position of sufficient influence to take over top philanthropic responsibilities. There is often a decided relationship between a man's rise to the top positions in charitable campaigns and his rise in the business hierarchy. Many business enterprises now include "training" for such community responsibilities.

Some corporations feel, also, that philanthropy serves as important training in salesmanship, and urge their staffs to take part. As control of philanthropic activity has changed from religious institutions and the upper classes to business, it is not unusual to find that family position is not now as important as formerly in obtaining high positions in philanthropic activity. Today it is considered almost essential to have a business organization behind the leader of a fund-raising campaign, for his firm can look after his work during the campaign and furnish him additional staff. He can also use his firm's name to get subscriptions and personnel.

ity, recognition, immortality, and belonging, for as John Donne phrases it "No man is an island entire of itself; every man is a piece of the continent, a part of the main."

Edward Streeter, banker and author, has answered better than most the question of why men give. It is contained in his essay, "The Harvard I Remember," read at a class agents' dinner: "I read Jim Conant's excellent reports. I look at the pictures of cyclotrons in the Alumni Bulletin. I am proud to be associated with such a terrific place. But I don't really understand it very well. So when I am asked for my ante each year by Bob Storer, let me confess that I do not really give to the new Harvard, which I scarcely comprehend, but to the old Harvard, which I loved." [9]

The meaning of philanthropy was expressed by John D. Rockefeller, III: "Meaning literally 'love of man,' philanthropy has its origins deep in our Judeo-Christian heritage, which teaches that each man has a responsibility toward his fellows. . . . Philanthropy, we should remember, involves more than the giving of money: it includes the contribution of one's self, of one's time, thought, and energy, as well as material resources." [16] Mr. Rockefeller stressed that the true meaning of the word *philanthropy* should guide and motivate each individual's giving.

REFERENCES CHAPTER 5

1. Anger, Charles A.: Fund-raising public relations generates generosity for charity, Spot Magazine, May, 1957.

2. Annual Report: Merrill, Lynch, Pierce, Fenner and Beane, 1957.

3. Berne, Eric: Games People Play, The Psychology of Human Relationships, New York, Grove, 1964.

4. Bonhoeffer, Dietrich: Ethics, New York, Macmillan, 1955, p. 21.

5. Clark, J. Reuben, Jr.: Church Welfare Plan. A Discussion, Salt Lake City General Church Welfare Comm of the Church of Jesus Christ of Latter-Day Saints, 1939.

6. Cleveland Plain Dealer: March 31, 1965.

7. Development Dynamics: Philanthropic Papers, No. 10, New York, John Price Jones Company, 30 East 42nd Street, April 15, 1964.

8. Dichter, Ernest: Why People Give, New York, United Community Funds and Councils of America, 1956.

9. Fellows, Margaret, and Koenig, Stella A.: Tested Methods of Raising Money, New York, Harper, 1959.

10. Fundamentals of Cultivating Key-Gift Prospects for a College Capital Campaign. Philanthropic Papers, No. 5, *ibid.*, ref. 7, Oct. 2, 1963.

11. Giving, USA: A Compilation of Facts Related to American Philanthropy, New York, Amer Ass of Fund-Raising Counsel, 1967.

12. Lauterbach, Albert: Man, Motives, and Money. Psychological Frontiers of Economics, ed. 2, Ithaca (NY), Cornell Univ Press, 1959.

13. Niebuhr, Reinhold: The Nature and Destiny of Man, vol. 2, New York, Scribner's, 1953, p. 43.

14. Personal communication.

15. Powell, Luther P.: Money and the Church, New York, Ass Press, 1962.

16. Rockefeller, John D., III: Address before the Fed of Jewish Philanthropies of New York, October 4, 1964.

17. Seymour, Harold J.: Fundamentals of Special Gifts Work in Capital Campaigns. One of a series of occasional memoranda for clients and friends, October 23, 1947.

18. ———: We support as we believe, YMCA Magazine, February, 1952, pp. 12-13.

19. Some of the Who . . . Why . . . and How . . . of Giving: Bull Amer Ass of Fund-Raising Counsel, vol. 7, October, 1961.

20. Van Dusen, Henry P.: They Found the Church There, New York, Scribner, 1945.

Altruism and Money

MUCH OF OUR SHARING with others comes, directly or indirectly, through money. So much of our hope for survival in this nuclear age rests on our altruistic love that money and altruism not only belong together but must not be separated without considerable misuse of both. Aristotle taught that the true nature of anything is the highest that it can become. Accepting this, one finds that altruism is not foreign to man's nature. One need not insist that the individual is born altruistic; he need believe only that he is born with a capacity for altruism.

A. S. Neill, who has directed Summerhill School, in England, for over forty years, says that every child is an egoist, but that if he is allowed to live out his egoism then it gradually widens to include a concern for others.[14] Erich Fromm expresses his conviction that education must be geared to the psychic needs and capacities of children, as they are not born altruists, nor do they love with the mature love of an adult. Thus one should not expect an early development of altruism, but look for its emergence after childhood.[7]

Altruism is devotion to the welfare of others, regard for others as a principle of action. It is the direct opposite of egoism or selfishness, in which interest in one's own welfare to the exclusion of others' remains the guiding principle of action. One of my responsibilities at Tulane School of Medicine is to conduct personal interviews with hundreds of students who want to study medicine. About every third student will mention altruism as a part of his motivation for wanting to enter the medical profession, though often he will apologize for introducing a motive that seems suspect today.

Discussing this topic with psychiatrists, I find that many share the conviction that the development of altruism in a patient is a sign of improvement in therapy in any age group. Psychiatrist Alfred Adler stressed the development of social consciousness as evidence of maturing. Adler's focus on social interest (*Gemein-schaftsgefühl*) as a criterion for mental health has led some critics to label him superficial. Beyond question, however, an adequate definition of mental health must include a deep feeling of identification, sympathy and affection for human beings in general, and a genuine desire to help mankind.* The development of social concern is in keeping with the highest precepts of ethics and religion, and also offers a wholesome corrective to some of the dreary materialistic pictures of man that have been popular for the past half-century. Fortunately, there is a revival of interest in the studies that find man endowed with altruism, humanitarianism, cooperation, creativity, and awareness. Such positive social adjustment reflects a highly developed capacity for social interest and is not solely the conquest of selfish forces by social forces.[1-2]

Social interest as an innate potentiality can be devel-

---

* A challenging testimony to the value of such a philosophy was recently given to the Yale freshmen by President Kingman Brewster, Jr.: "The fullness or emptiness of life will be measured by the extent to which a man feels that he has an impact on the lives of others. To be a man is to matter to someone outside yourself, or to some calling or cause bigger than yourself."

oped only when the child is in the midst of life, in the social context. The development of the capacity for co-operation and altruistic endeavors occurs first in the mother-child relationships. The mother is the first "other" being whom the child experiences. Under her care, he makes an ever-widening circle of human contacts. If, however, the mother focuses the child's social interest on herself, she will thwart the extension of his interest to others. This may become a crucial factor in the development of the person who, lacking other-directedness, becomes enclosed in a small social circle.

Clinical evidence continues to indicate that the individual's capacity for cooperation, collaboration, compromise and generosity unfolds naturally when there are conducive life situations.[20] Freud said to Ludwig Binswanger: "I have always restricted my study and work to the basement and groundfloor of the edifice called man." That is no reflection on Freud, but it is in some sense a continuation of his work that we move on to study the upper floors.

SELFISHNESS AND SELF-LOVE

The question is often raised of the difference, if any, between selfishness and self-love. Love for others and love for self are not mutually exclusive. The biblical admonition to "love thy neighbor as thyself" implies that respect and love for another individual cannot be separated from respect and love for one's self. In fact, present-day psychiatry insists that love for one's self is inseparably connected with the love for another being. Erich Fromm has stated this well:

From this it follows that my own self must be as much an object of my love as another person. The affirmation of one's own life, happiness, growth, freedom is rooted in one's capacity to love, i.e., in care, respect, responsibility and knowledge. If an individual is able to love productively, he loves himself too, if he can love only others, he cannot love at all.[7]

It is sometimes forgotten that to be a man means to be a fellow man. The personality becomes *human* through its association with others, for man fulfills himself in human relationships. He has drives for affiliations as well as for destruction. Even if one concedes that every act of care for another person is only care for the self one projects into another, one is still capable of giving acceptance that is significant to that other person. If all love is self-love, it could be said that humanity is really one and that empathy reflects the primordial unity of which all were originally a part.[10] The biblical scholar Leo Baeck[4] has given a somewhat different translation of Leviticus 19:18, usually translated "Thou shalt love thy neighbor as thyself." The exact translation, he contends, would read, "Thou shalt love thy other; he is as thou." Thus, one loves his neighbor because his neighbor is like him.

The selfish person is interested only in himself. He wants everything for himself and derives no pleasure from giving, only from taking. He looks on the world mostly from the standpoint of what he can get out of it. Psychoanalytic studies reveal that the selfish person does not love himself too much, but too little. His appearing to care too much for himself is really an attempt to cover up and compensate for his failure to care for his real self. It is usually recognized that selfish persons are incapable of loving others, but often overlooked that they are also incapable of loving themselves.

Much about the nature of selfishness has been learned by psychoanalytic experience with neurotic "unselfishness." Such an "unselfish" patient wants nothing for himself, lives for others, and is proud that he considers himself unimportant. In spite of his "unselfishness," he is unhappy and puzzled by his discontent. His relationships to those closest to him are also unsatisfactory. This person usually presents symptoms such as depression, fatigue and inability to work. Psychoanalytic exploration of the psyche of such a person reveals that behind the facade of unselfishness, a subtle and intense self-centeredness is hidden. This person can be healed only when he recognizes his so-called "unselfishness" for what it is, and acquires an understanding and acceptance of self-love. A section in *Meister Eckhart* contributes meaningfully to this discussion:

If you love yourself, you love everybody else as you do yourself. As long as you love another person less than you love yourself, you will not really succeed in loving yourself, but if you love all alike, including yourself, you will love them as one person and that person is both God and man. Thus he is a great and righteous person who, loving himself, loves all others equally.[18]

THE POWER OF LOVE

As man in his development moved away from a simple life close to the earth and broke his primary bonds with nature, he experienced a separateness, an isolation, an aloneness. He has since tried to overcome his separateness and find "at-onement." By trial and error, man through the centuries has discovered that love banishes his isolation and separateness, reunites him with his fellows, and yet permits him to retain his identity and integrity. In all relationships, giving is a major component. Herein, one of the great paradoxes of life is found: in love, giving means receiving. In love, one gives himself. As Fromm has said, "This does not necessarily mean that he sacrifices his life for the other—but that he gives him of that which is alive in him; he gives him of his joy, of his interest, of his understanding, of his knowledge, of his humor, of his sadness—of all expressions and manifestations of that which is alive in him." [7]

In giving his love, he enriches the other person and enhances the other's sense of aliveness. By giving, one cannot help bringing something to life in the other person, and that which is brought to life reflects back to him. Thus, in giving one cannot help receiving, although one gives with no such thing in mind. Giving often makes the other person a giver, as both the giver and receiver share in the joy of what they have brought to life. The spirit of such an encounter has been beautifully described by James Russell Lowell: "Be noble! and the nobleness that lies in other men, sleeping, but never dead, will rise in majesty to meet thine own."

Man discovered long ago that love is a power that produces love. Of course, the ability to love as an act of giving depends on the character development of the person. He must have overcome his dependency, his narcissism, his wish to exploit others and his tendency to hoard. He must also have acquired faith in his own powers and courage to rely on them in the attainment of his goals.

Fromm defines love as the active concern for the life and the growth of that which we love. He emphasizes that beyond the element of giving, the active character of love becomes evident in that it always implies certain basic elements common to all forms of love: care, responsibility, respect, and knowledge.[7] All of these elements of love, with the possible exception of knowledge, are readily seen as related to altruism. An examination of knowledge will show its crucial relevance also. One of the major concerns of man is expressed in the Delphic motto: "Know thyself." This quest to know ourselves by penetrating into the secret of man's soul is the mainspring of psychology. The biological aspects of life are a miracle and a secret, and man in his human aspects is an unfathomable secret to himself and to his fellow man. Fromm calls our attention to the fact that the basic need to fuse with another person so as to transcend the prison of one's separateness is closely related to another specifically human desire, to know the "secret of man." [7] Approaches used to probe the "secret of man" have been: *a*. through domination, which transforms the person into a thing one possesses; *b*. through sadism, which forces the person to betray the "secret of life" in suffering; and *c*. through love, which is based on the concept of human solidarity, of the oneness of all mankind.

The attempt to exercise complete power and domination over another human being may lead to extreme sadism. In the craving for penetrating man's secret may be found an essential motivation for the depth and intensity of cruelty and destructiveness. This idea has been expressed succinctly by Isaac Babel, quoting a fellow officer in the Russian Civil War who had just stamped his former master to death: "With shooting— I'll put it this way—with shooting you only get rid of a chap. . . . With shooting you'll never get at the soul, to where it is in a fellow and how it shows itself. But I don't spare myself, and I've more than once trampled an enemy for over an hour. You see, I want to get to know what life really is, what life's like down our way." [8]

Why does the Bible urge us to love the stranger, the poor, the widow and the orphan? One reason may be that in the love of those who do not serve a purpose, love begins to unfold. Love for the helpless and the frail seems intimately related to the love of oneself and one's brother. "Love ye therefore the stranger: for ye were strangers in the land of Egypt" (Deuteronomy 10:19). Who among us has not at some time been a stranger in the land of Egypt? Thus in the mature individual, compassion implies an element of identification. Altruistic acts then follow in a natural and spontaneous manner.

In searching for the extent to which man can be altruistic, Reinhold Niebuhr's brilliant work is helpful.[15] He stresses the two paradoxical facts about man. First, man is a child of nature, subject to its vicissitudes, compelled by its necessities, and driven by its impulses. Second, man is a spirit who stands outside of nature. Created in the image of God, man has transcendence over nature. As Niebuhr understands this, the image refers to man's capacity for self-transcendence, to man's capacity to make an object of himself. It gives man a capacity for objectivity, viewing himself as an object, appraising the degree to which this "object" acts as he would wish to be acted toward. In this ability and this inborn "golden rule" Niebuhr finds the source of morality, the root of conscience. The law of man's nature is love, pointed to by man's self-transcendence. The inevitable condition of man is anxiety, but if he trusts in God, he believes his anxious state God-intended. His anxiety becomes, therefore, the energy of creativity: infinite possibilities come as challenges and act as leaven for humble achievement.

ALIENATED MAN AND ALTRUISM

Much is said of man's aloneness today. The processes of individualism, competition and stratification act to interfere with meaningful communication and inhibit man's ability to establish lasting contact with his fellows. The aged, single, unemployed, sick and physically handicapped, especially, encounter isolating circumstances.

How do men isolated by modern society react, either consciously or unconsciously, to the isolating processes? What efforts do they make to relate themselves to others?[22] One may become a "wanderer" and travel to the ends of the earth, enjoying freedom from responsibility and the joy of discovery. Another may become a lonely egotist in his attempt to escape the isolation engendered by his own sense of insecurity and inferiority. His course may lead from minor idiosyncrasies to neuroses, or from alcoholism to suicide, the egotist's despairing admission of total surrender to his isolation. One can also deal with his isolation by becoming an authoritarian escapist. Such a person's isolation stems from his inability to establish relationships that will provide him with recognition, status and a feeling of personal worth within the community. The authoritarian escapist can be hidebound by authoritarian attitudes or possess an irrational subservience to authority.

Isolated man attempts to overcome his aloneness in two other ways. One is that of the envious individual who tries to mitigate his own misfortune by impairing the good fortune of another. The other technique an isolated person may use is to compensate for his handicap by making an effort to do something worthy of recognition. These two courses are mentioned in Sir Francis Bacon's *Of Envy:*

For he that cannot possibly mend his own case, will do what he can to impair another's; except these defects light upon a very brave and heroical nature, which thinketh to make his natural wants part of his honour, in that it should be said, "That an eunuch, or a lame man, did such great matters"; affecting the honour of a miracle.

Fortunately for society, many men suffering from a sense of isolation and exile lose themselves in altruistic service to mankind. The psychological term for drawing strength from one's weakness, or responding creatively to some handicap, is called compensation. The key to the compensatory process is forgetting self in the service of others. True forgetfulness of self in altruism means rising above any bitterness and resentment that may have been engendered by the isolating role of dependency, inferiority, aloneness or scorn from which the sufferer is trying to deliver himself. Of course, the question is painfully asked, "How can we forget ourselves when we are so important to ourselves?"

The ancient Greeks' familiarity with this forgetting of self is dramatically symbolized in the Homeric story of the wound and the bow, dealt with in Sophocles' great drama *Philoctetes*.[21] A poisonous snake bites Philoctetes when he and his companions stop at Chrysa on their way to Troy. The wound refuses to heal, festers and gives off a horrid odor. The repulsiveness of the wound, combined with Philoctetes' agonizing groans, lead his shipmates, at the instigation of Odysseus, to abandon him. When the ship stops at the lonely island of Lemnos, he is transferred to land while he is asleep, and his ship sails to Troy without him. Time passes and the Greeks learn through an oracle that they cannot win the war against Troy without the wonder-working bow of Heracles. As it happens, the wounded and abandoned Philoctetes has the bow in his possession. Odysseus assumes that the suffering and embittered Philoctetes will not part with the bow willingly. Thus he returns to Lemnos, hoping to secure the bow by trickery. Odysseus chooses Neoptolemus, an honest youth, to wheedle the bow from Philoctetes. Neoptolemus refuses to take advantage of him and reveals the plot. In spontaneous altruism, Philoctetes conquers his deep resentment and offers the bow to help his countrymen. The moment he bestows the gift, his "one talent," his wound is miraculously healed and he is able to take a crucial part in the siege of Troy.

Sophocles is here iterating the basic elements of the compensatory process: *a.* the cankerous wound that will not heal, *b.* the bitter isolation, *c.* the bestowing of the gift, *d.* the healing of the wound, and *e.* the inclusion once more in the group. We recognize the same compensatory elements today. Our isolation vanishes when we reintegrate ourselves through altruism into the family of man. The power of love to heal a man's alienation and aloneness, and to break down the barriers that separate him from his neighbor is highlighted by J. C. F. von Schiller:

> Have Love. Not love alone for one,
> But man as man thy brother call;
> And scatter like the circling sun
> Thy charities on all.

Readers who want to investigate further the subject of altruism should become familiar with the work of Pitirim A. Sorokin and the Harvard Research Center in Creative Altruism. Sorokin's experimental studies claim for unselfish love the most enormous creative and therapeutic potentialities. They see it as a life-giving force, necessary for physical, mental and moral health.[19] The supreme value of love, the veritable *mysterium tremendum et fascinosum*, was intuited long ago by the inspired apostles of love, by the great moral teachers of humanity, by founders of all genuine religions, by the great sages, seers, and prophets of practically all countries, cultures and periods. In terms such as love, altruism, benevolence, *Eros, Agape,* and the Golden Rule, they have affirmed supreme love as the highest moral value and its imperatives as the universal and perennial moral commandments. Sorokin stresses that this supreme moral value has been recognized and prescribed by all social groups in human history.[17-19] Desmonde's studies regarding the origin of money,[5] mentioned in other chapters of this book, offer a historical dimension relevant to Sorokin's findings.

The most urgent need of man is the transcendence of all tribal solidarities by the uinversal solidarity of mankind through creative ennoblement of man's nature. The attainment of such a goal is not a utopian dream; to survive, man must achieve it. The nuclear age has destroyed the boundary lines of tribes and clans and catapulted man into membership in one community. He has not been prepared for this membership, or for the acceptance of all men as his brothers; yet he must become a member of the family of man or be destroyed. His path of survival is through extending to all men the creative altruism that, until now, has extended to only his own tiny social unit. Brock G. Chisholm, psychiatrist and WHO leader, for years has stressed that the limiting loyalties that most of us learned in childhood may be preventing our developing new behavior patterns appropriate to and necessary for survival in our new era.

GROWTH TOWARD ALTRUISM

Psychologists such as Abraham Maslow are formulating a new concept of health and sickness in human beings.[8-9, 12, 16] Using studies of average and healthy persons, Maslow has demonstrated that human beings can be loving, noble, creative, and capable of pursuing the highest values and aspirations. In *his own nature*, man demonstrates a pressure toward a more nearly perfect humanity in the same way that an acorn presses toward becoming an oak tree.

Man is ultimately not molded or shaped into humanness, or taught to be human. The role of the environment is ultimately to permit him or help him to actualize his own potentialities, not its potentialities. The environment does not give him potentialities and capacities; he has them in inchoate or embryonic form, just exactly as he has embryonic arms and legs. And creativeness, spontaneity, selfhood, authenticity, caring for others, being able to love, yearning for truth are embryonic potentialities belonging to his species-membership just as much as are his arms and legs.[12]

Maslow is not contradicting the mass of data, which shows clearly that living in a family and in a culture are absolutely necessary to actualize the psychological potentials that make man human. The teacher and the culture do not create a human being or implant within him the ability to love, share or to be curious and creative. Rather, they permit and encourage what exists in embryo to become real and actual. Thus, culture can be compared to sun, food and water, but never to seed.

A general motivation theory compatible with what has already been stressed centers on the theory of need gratification. The principle that binds together the variety of human motives is the tendency for a new and higher need to emerge as the lower need fulfills itself by being sufficiently gratified.[11] As the child grows, normally he becomes satiated and bored with the delights that he has savored sufficiently in each psychosocial stage of development. Eagerly, and without pushing, he goes on to higher and more complex delights as they become available to him without danger or threat.

The growth process stops or regresses only when he suffers frustration, ridicule, failure or disapproval. When that happens, neurotic tendencies begin to develop, and the individual is in bondage to a number of emotionally unhealthy characteristics and compromises. If the growth process is allowed to develop normally and naturally, the end result is a self-actualizing person. He moves toward the realization of his potentialities as a person. After he attains the gratification of one basic need, that gratification opens consciousness to domination by another "higher" need. Thus he moves ever upward, pausing in his growth to enjoy "peak experiences," which give him a glimpse of the ultimate, of the, for him, absolute.

CONCLUSION

The question invariably asked regarding altruism is, "What are the person's motives?" A variety of viewpoints are expressed by any group of individuals, ranging from self-centeredness to spontaneous and fulfilling love. To some extent the question is more academic than practical. Even the words of St. Francis, "for it is in giving that we receive," may be subjected to a critical analysis as to motive, as also Lowell's, from "The Vision of Sir Launfal":

> The gift without the giver is bare;
> Who gives himself with his alms feeds three,—
> Himself, his hungering neighbor and me.

One's own view in regard to motivation is related in large to his orientation about the nature and destiny of man.

Much of the material here points toward an intrinsic quality of altruism in man that easily blossoms if given an opportunity to develop. The view of psychologists such as Maslow differs from the classical psychoanalytic position as represented, for example, by Anna Freud:

It remains an open question whether there is such a thing as a genuinely altruistic relation to one's fellow-man, in which the gratification of one's own instinct plays no part at all, even in some displaced and sublimated form. In any case it is certain that projection and identification are not the only means of acquiring an attitude which has every appearance of altruism; for instance, another and easy route to the same goal is by way of the various forms of masochism.[6]

Probably as we learn more about the origin and development of conscience, we will learn more about altruism. Much of the code of conscience is developed through a process of socialization. There is another element in conscience that relates to the nature of man, which Maslow identifies as "intrinsic conscience."[12] This is based, at the deepest level of awareness, on the perception of our own nature, of our own destiny, of our own capacities, of our own call in life. This intrinsic conscience insists that we be true to our inner self, and that we do not deny it out of weakness or for special advantage. When we bury our talents or refuse to take a stand in the presence of social injustice, we perceive on some level that we have done wrong to ourselves and we often dislike ourselves for it.

The truth-revealing techniques, such as education and psychotherapy, lessen hostility, fear and greed, and increase love, courage, creativeness and altruism. This leads one to conclude that love and the latter qualities are "deeper," more natural and more basic than hostility and the former. Thus, what one calls "bad" behavior is lessened or removed, while what one calls "good" behavior is strengthened and fostered, by uncovering.

Although at times one can destroy or exploit others, his tendency still is to bind up the wounds of his neighbor, to replant his fields destroyed by flood or war, to help and to interact with him constructively. It seems essential in all work, regardless of one's vocation, that altruism be kept alive and untarnished. If it is, then the cynicism prevalent today will give way to a tradition of geniune service, guided by love, the willingness to share, and the feeling of solidarity with all mankind.

REFERENCES CHAPTER 6

1. Adler, Alfred: *In* Ansbacher, H. L., and Ansbacher, R. R., eds.: Superiority and Social Interest. A Collection of Later Writings, Evanston, Northwestern Univ Press, 1964.

2. Ansbacher, H. L., and Ansbacher, R. R., eds.: The Individual Psychology of Alfred Adler, New York, Basic, 1956.

3. Babel, Isaac: The Collected Stories, New York, Criterion Book, 1955.

4. Baeck, Leo: The Essence of Judaism, translated by Irving Howe, New York, Schocken, 1948.

5. Desmonde, William H.: Magic, Myth, and Money. The Origin of Money in Religious Ritual, New York, Free Press, 1962.

6. Freud, Anna: The Ego and the Mechanisms of Defense, translated by Cecil Baines, New York, Internat Univ Press, 1946.

7. Fromm, Erich: The Art of Loving, New York, Harper, 1956.

8. Jourard, Sidney M.: Personal Adjustment. An Approach Through the Study of Healthy Personality, ed. 2, New York, Macmillan, 1963.

9. ———: The Transparent Self, Princeton (NJ), Van Nostrand, 1964.

10. Katz, Robert L.: Empathy. Its Nature and Uses, New York, Free Press, 1963.

11. Maslow, Abraham H.: Motivation and Personality, New York, Harper, 1954.

12. ———: Toward a Psychology of Being, Princeton (NJ), Van Nostrand, 1962.

13. Meister Eckhart: Translated by R. B. Blakney, New York, Harper, 1941, p. 204.

14. Neill, A. S.: Summerhill: A Radical Approach to Child Rearing, New York, Hart Pub, 1960.

15. Niebuhr, Reinhold: The Nature and Destiny of Man, New York, Scribner, 1941-1943.

16. Rogers, Carl R.: On Becoming a Person, Boston, Houghton, 1961.

17. Sorokin, Pitirim A.: Social and Cultural Dynamics, Boston, Extending Horizons Press, 1957.

18. ———: Social Philosophies of an Age of Crisis, Boston, Beacon Press, 1950.

19. ———: The Ways and Power of Love, Boston, Beacon Press, 1954.

20. Sullivan, Harry Stack: Conceptions of Modern Psychiatry, New York, Norton, 1940.

21. Wilson, Edmund: The Wound and the Bow, Cambridge (Mass), Harvard Univ Press, 1941.

22. Wood, Margaret Mary: Paths of Loneliness. The Individual Isolated in Modern Society, New York, Columbia Univ Press, 1953.

Money and the Quest for the Grail

A PEACE CORPS volunteer said to me that he was committed to Peace Corps principles and that his family was committed to the same philosophy. I was interviewing him—I am a psychiatric consultant to the Peace Corps—to assess his motivation for undertaking a difficult assignment overseas. He said that almost the whole world seemed committed to acquiring money as an end in itself, when actually money had no meaning except as a medium of communicating, of sharing and expressing one's kinship and solidarity with other people, and that service in the Peace Corps exemplified the basic conviction of his family that each man must earn his membership in the family of man through being human in its finest sense. As I listened, I heard Teilhard de Chardin, great scientist and theologian, say again: "It is because the earth is round that we have become human: you see we could not get away, we could not help but rub against each other."

Empirical studies seem to confirm that man's deepest happiness stems from his identification with the creative energies of nature, through which he dedicates himself to the advancement of civilization. This Peace Corps volunteer was expressing a viewpoint similar to that of social philosophers such as William H. Desmonde, who emphasizes that money should be thought of as a symbol of grace.[1] Grace, then, can be seen as the awakening within a person of insight into his own nature, as well as divine inspiration.

In the biblical tradition, grace refers to the bestowal of a kindness that could not have been claimed, or to the unmerited kindness thus bestowed. While much of the religious terminology of the Old Testament is borrowed from covenantal and legal practice (man or God must or will act in a certain way because of a contractual agreement), there is also present the belief that God will do more for man than he deserves (Exodus 34:6-7; II Chron. 30:9; Neh. 9:17, 31; Joel 2:13; Psalms 86:15). In New Testament language, grace has the simple and general meaning of favor shown or received and the disposition to show favor, hence liberality, agreeableness (Luke 1:30; 2:40, 52; 6:32-34; Acts 2:47). Grace is, further, the divine help continually given by which man is kept and sustained, and enabled to do what is otherwise beyond his power (II Cor. 12:9).

Money originated in some ancient cultures as a religious symbol in sacrificial food communion rituals.[1] Participation in the sacrificial meal signified the commitment of the individual to a bond of loyalty with the other members of the group, and meant also entering into a covenant with the deity. The particular portion of the sacrificial flesh that the communicant received and his position at the feast signified his standing in the community.

With the establishment of the market economy, the quest for grace, originally symbolized by the cult symbols, tended to become transformed into the quest for money.[1,4] At first, the establishment of a contractual relationship between two individuals retained traces of the original bond of religious loyalty among members of the same communion, with impersonal bargaining replacing the patriarchal redistribution of goods among the brotherhood. With the change in religion's values, the possession of money tended to be regarded as a social honor, regardless of whether the individual had made a worthwhile contribution to the welfare of the community.

The basic emotional yearning of the healthy individual is for freely given devotion to the advancement of human welfare. The individual feels most fulfilled when he is able to abandon himself in mutual sharing with the past, present and future members of society. Desmonde's extensive study on the origin of money in religious ritual concludes that the fulfillment of this basic emotional need may be regarded as the true function of money—a giving and receiving springing from one's innermost self out of a deep sense of joy and abundance.

The quest for unity is the oldest of mankind's aspirations, for it is the deepest of all our yearnings. Money in this respect is the longing for true love. Although money has failed to achieve this unity, all of us feel this sense of oneness occasionally, as for example when we perform a charitable act, or when, like primitive people, we exchange gifts among our kinship group.[1]

In the biblical concept of the love of money as the root of all evil, the admonition is against surrendering oneself to what would endanger the unique creaturely life and its personal unity, which God has called his *creation*. If one runs away from his personhood, or from being a child of God, and attaches himself in some way to an authority that then becomes master, he is subjecting himself to an evil or destructive power. Instead of controlling and integrating material things into his personal and orderly world, he comes to be dominated by them. Thus enters a special form of corruption—the worship of power for its own sake and the pursuit of the common road to power, namely *money*.

Unfortunately, money in modern society does not often symbolize well the great tradition of love, grace, and service. T. S. Eliot's *The Waste Land* may be said to express the feeling of hollowness symbolized by many of the modern uses and misuses of money. Hollowness results from the absence in our civilization of a set of cultural goals and purposes that impart enthusiasm to life, love, and work. According to Eliot's own notes, much of the symbolism of *The Waste Land* comes from Jessie L. Weston's book on the Grail legend, *From Ritual to Romance*.[5] One reads there that "when the land becomes waste . . . the task of the hero is that of restoration."

The substance of Eliot's poem is a moral revulsion against the sterilities of a materialist culture. Eliot attempts to imbue a sense of the sordidness and vulgarity, the moral debility and spiritual desiccation of modern life. The title of the poem is taken from a medieval legend about a parched land ruled over by an infirm and maimed Fisher King, the fate of whose land is bound up with his. Until he is healed, the land remains under a curse. The curse may be removed only when a knight makes his way to the castle of the Fisher King and actively seeks truth by demanding the meaning of the various symbols displayed there. Only then would be revealed to the knight the secret doctrine that death and birth are interrelated and that the way into life is through death.

For the reader, the employment of the wasteland legend has a special relevance. Eliot is attempting to dramatize what it feels like to live in a secularized world, a world emptied of religious meaning. A prime difficulty, however, for the present-day reader is that he is himself often too thoroughly secularized to comprehend what the poet is talking about. Eliot adopts the device of putting the reader into something like the position of the knight in the legend of the Holy Grail. According to the story, the knight was able to remove the curse only if he questioned what he saw, only if he demanded meanings of the symbols shown him. The truth was not revealed to him if he merely wondered at the meanings of the symbols.

Although *The Waste Land* emphasizes our civilization in the winter of its discontent, its central concern is the regenerative power of life, the spring and its new fruit, the laborious process of rebirth. The curse upon the land relates to the unwillingness to give oneself, to make a positive commitment. The antidote to the curse lies in the ability to give, to sympathize and to surrender to something outside the self in an attempt to transcend one's essential isolation.

One of the most important traditions in the western world is exemplified in the chivalric tales of King Arthur and the Knights of the Round Table. Encompassed in the quest for the Holy Grail were those genuine goals of character—altruism, loyalty, courage, and religious devotion. A persistent motif in the Arthurian legends focuses on a blight upon the land resulting from the weakening of the king. Vitality can be restored only by finding the Holy Grail. Seeking for the sacred vessel is actually a type of initiation in which the seeker's task is to find the source of grace and energy lacking both in the country and within himself.

The behavioral sciences would interpret "the blight upon the land" as the lack of the feeling of belonging, the absence of social cohesion and higher dedication. By establishing feelings of genuine friendship and emotional commitment, the sense of futility and meaninglessness could be removed from the land. Thus, to a great extent, the knight's quest for the Holy Grail was really a search for emotional warmth and fellowship, for a sense of solidarity and community with all mankind.

Today, many are aware of their emptiness, and long for something that will fill them with a zest for living, with wholeness, with a sense of belonging. Such people often seek an antidote for their emptiness through the acquisition of more and more money. The acquisition of money ends in stultification when individuals lose sight of the true meaning of money—the expression of loyalty in economic relations. Then the scriptural reminder, "to whom much is given, much is required," stands in judgment upon accumulation as an end in itself.

Many uses of money may be emotionally and neurotically determined. Money is a means to an end, not an end *per se*. Through it one acquires certain things he needs and desires. One does not allow himself to be taken advantage of in money matters, but tries to make money as best he can, without sacrificing either health, love, hobbies, recreation, or life goals to this end. Money does not become the center of life with everything else subordinated to the "urge" to possess money. Normally, money has no infantile strings attached to it, and is not a blind for repressed infantile conflicts. Spending money is taken for granted; no "surgical operation" is required to separate a dollar from its owner and put the dollar in circulation. The possession or hoarding of money does not become paramount. Unjustified demands for money are necessarily warded off in a matter-of-fact way, nor do such demands generate fury, excitement or indignation. The phrase "I cannot afford it" is a simple statement of an objective fact.

At no time should money be allowed to obscure or blur one's basic commitment to the great tradition of love, grace, and service. To live in a world where men do not love, and where they use money to cheat and to destroy, is to have a foretaste of hell. Fortunately in some areas of modern life, such as the world of the arts, wealth is spent in return for spiritual enrichment. Also, the realization that man lives by more than what is bought and sold is dawning on many people. President John F. Kennedy once eloquently expressed a hope shared by many of his fellow countrymen: "I look forward to an America which will not be afraid of grace and beauty . . ."

A recent novel, *God Bless You, Mr. Rosewater*, contemplates the unusual ways in which many Americans regard money.[3] The despair of Vonnegut, the author, is based on substitution of automated charity for love.

Automated charity actually is a poor substitute for brotherly concern or what could be designated as empathy. Money can become, when properly used, an empathic instrument. Where there is empathy there is real understanding of the other as a person. We understand his suffering in relationship to his personal and social world; we share, we feel *for* him and *with* him. To describe such a relationship, the German psychologist Theodor Lipps used the word *Einfühlung* ("in-feeling"). Others have described empathy in human relationships by stating that a man will do unto others as he would have them do unto him because he will feel their feelings as he does his own. Money once had an important role in nurturing such a relationship, and to some extent, such a role still exists. The urgent need is to recapture this original condition.

In all our actions, and especially our use of money, Einstein's analysis of our relatedness to all mankind furnishes the perspective we need:

Strange is our situation here upon earth. Each of us comes for a short visit, not knowing why, yet sometimes seeming to divine a purpose. From the standpoint of daily life, however, there is one thing we know: That Man is here for the sake of other Men. . . . Above all, for those upon whose smile and well-being our own happiness depends, and also for the countless unknown souls with whose fate we are connected by a bond of sympathy. Many times a day I realize how much my own outer and inner life is built upon the labors of my fellow men, both living and dead, and how earnestly I must exert myself in order to give in return as much as I have received.[2]

Man is becoming more sensitive to man and to the whole of creation. He is experimenting more and more with going out of his individual self into the service of others. Man need not walk upon an alien earth. In his interior evolution change is evident, especially in his understanding of his own spiritual relationships. Henry David Thoreau's analysis seems sound: "Why has man rooted himself thus firmly in the earth, but that he may rise in the same proportion into the heavens above?"

REFERENCES CHAPTER 7

1. Desmonde, William H.: Magic, Myth, and Money. The Origin of Money in Religious Ritual, New York, Free Press, 1962.
2. Einstein, Albert: Quoted by Harold Stevens: Humor plus humility equals humaneness, JAMA *190*:1117, 1964.
3. Vonnegut, Kurt, Jr.: God Bless You, Mr. Rosewater, New York, Holt, 1965.
4. Weber, Max: The Protestant Ethic and the Spirit of Capitalism, translated by Talcott Parsons, London, George Allen and Unwin, Ltd., 1950.
5. Weston, Jessie L.: From Ritual to Romance, London, Cambridge, 1920.

Index

180

Index 181

182 FOR THE LOVE OF MONEY

demption from, 30; spending
and, 49

Hanson, Abel, 132
Herzog, Elizabeth, 85
Hoarding, by child, 93
Holy Grail, money and, 172
Humanitarianism, 131
Hunt, Herold C., 129
Hustler(s), 78-79

Immortality, money and, 31
Imposter(s), 78-79
Injury, fear of, 23
Insecurity, 54, 93
Isolation, 27, 162-164

Jaspan, Norman, 79
Jones, Ernest, 39, 41, 43, 46
Jones, James, 69
Josselyn, Irene M., 102, 112
Jourard, Sidney M., 83, 85, 170

Kane, Harnett T., 147
Katz, Robert L., 170
Kaufman, W., 52, 54, 56, 72, 85,
    86, 87, 96, 103, 113
Kennedy, John F., 178
Keynes, John M., 29, 32, 46
Kingsley, Charles, 33, 46
Kleptomania, 18
Koenig, Stella A., 154

Lauterbach, A., 46, 129, 150, 154
Lawrence, D. H., 114
Laziness, in child, 96
Lear, Martha W., 108, 113
Life, regenerative power, 176;
    secret of, 161; sharing, 24; zest
    for, 177
Lipps, Theodor, 178
Loewenstein, R. M., 30, 46, 70, 85
Love, bought, 120, 122; defini-
    tion, 160; giving and, 136;
    power of, 159-162, 165
Lowell, James Russell, 160, 168
Luther, Martin, 32

Marriage, money problems, 119
Masculinity, see Virility
Maslow, A., 166, 167, 169, 170
Masochism, in extractive behav-
    ior, 76; spending and, 53
Masturbation, gambling and, 60
Materialism, 83-84, 109, 175
Maugham, Somerset, 47
McCormick, Anne O'Hare, 151
Meadows, Algur H., 81, 82
Medders, Ernest, 80, 81
Meister Eckhart, 171
Mendenhall, James E., 129
Menninger, Karl, 132
Mental health, 156
Merrill, Charles, 130
Millionaire(s), 16
Miser(s), 21, 39, 55
Monetary strivings, 12-24
Money, adolescence and, 104-110;
    altruism, 155-177; as artificial
    wealth, 34; as bargaining agent,
    117; as excrement, 34-43; as
    goodluck charm, 72; as mana,
    20; as symbol of grace, 172, of
    masculinity, 120, of parental
    acceptance, 118; child-rearing
    and, 116-119; children and, 86-
    113; deprivation, 115, 116; em-
    pathy, 178; etymology of, 29;
    faith, 28; filthy, 32-45; immor-
    tality, 31; love bought with,
    120; love of, 21, 30, 174; marital
    discord and, 106, 115, 119-122;
    misuses of, 33, 47-85; male po-
    tency, 19; management of, 125;
    manipulative uses of, 68-72,
    117; origins of, 33, 173; patho-
    logical quest for, 25; power, 18;
    psychological meaning of, 11-
    46; psychosomatic illness, 83;
    115; punishment, 117; quest for
    Holy Grail, 172-179; redemp-
    tion, 30; responsibilities of, 87;
    revenge, 70; ritualistic uses of,
    72-73; secretiveness about, 83;
    social status, 29; superstition,